To Gain at Harvest

To Gain at Harvest

Portraits from the English Reformation

Jonathan Dean

scm press

© Jonathan Dean 2018

Published in 2018 by SCM Press
Editorial office
3rd Floor, Invicta House,
108–114 Golden Lane,
London EC1Y 0TG, UK

www.scmpress.co.uk

SCM Press is an imprint of Hymns Ancient & Modern Ltd (a registered
charity)

Hymns Ancient & Modern® is a registered trademark of Hymns Ancient &
Modern Ltd
13A Hellesdon Park Road, Norwich, Norfolk NR6 5DR, UK

The author and publisher acknowledge permission to reprint material from
the following sources:
T.S.Eliot, 1944 and 2001, 'Little Gidding', in Four Quartets, London: Faber &
Faber. Permission sought.
Nicola Slee, 2004, 'Conversations with Muse', in Praying Like a Woman,
London: SPCK

British Library Cataloguing in Publication data

A catalogue record for this book is available
from the British Library
978 0 334 05689 8

Printed and bound by CPI Group (UK) Ltd

Contents

I have found that things unknown have a secret influence on the soul, and like the centre of the earth unseen violently attract it. We love we know not what, and therefore everything allures us. As iron at a distance is drawn by the lodestone, there being some invisible communications between them, so is there in us a world of Love to somewhat, though we know not what in the world that should be. There are invisible ways of conveyance by which some great thing doth touch our souls, and by which we tend to it. Do you not feel yourself drawn with the expectation and desire of some Great Thing?

Thomas Traherne (*c.*1637–73), *Centuries* I, no. 2

Preface

About midday, on the Eve of All Saints', he strolled . . . the length of the little town, along the streets which to-morrow would be thronged with the faithful. He mounted the steps of the Schlosskirche and affixed his placard, as he had a right to do, and in the normal way: 'In the desire and with the purpose of elucidating the truth, a disputation will be held . . .'; at first sight no more exciting than most notices on most university boards. He turned away and went home, and no doubt ate a hearty meal.[1]

So Gordon Rupp's definitive account of *Luther's Progress to the Diet of Worms* describes the rather ordinary moment now credited with beginning the Protestant Reformation. Some historians doubt that this event took place in this way; others dispute that it happened at all; still others rightly contest the identification of this particular moment with the 'beginning' of a movement that was in fact multiple movements, with an array of expressions in a wide variety of places and contexts, and whose essential emphases, aims and ideas were already being discussed, debated and widely popularized long before 31 October 1517. Nevertheless, this was a seminal moment: when Martin Luther's growing distress and emerging dissent about some of the practices of the Roman Catholic Church found published form in a set of 95 'theses', or statements of claims he wished to be contested. Expecting simply an open debate, which he expected to be contained, localized and ultimately to justify his stance, he unleashed a whirlwind.

Over half a millennium since this event, as we recall the wider movements of which it was a part and which it fed into and augmented, Christians of all kinds are bound to reflect on the Reformations themselves, Protestant and Catholic, and on how they have shaped the Christian world since, both in life-giving and soul-destroying ways. Historians and theologians continue to contest what was really at stake, what the reformers were living and dying for and whether the effects of their revolution were intentional or not, foreseen or not, useful or not. Those believers who trace their faith's heritage in some senses to the sixteenth century might, ironically, have a much clearer and more definite sense of why they are Lutheran, Reformed, Catholic, Anglican or Baptist, and how these identities were forged in this time of testing and contesting: the primacy of the Scriptures, the need for connection between all Christians, the virtues of moderation, the cultivation of inner spiritual life over the practice of external actions, the importance of continuing communion with those who have gone before us, and so on. As I have argued elsewhere,[2] these senses of beginnings and inheritances, properly construed, are often neglected sources of life to the modern Church, which needs often to drink more deeply at the wellsprings of its own self-understanding, and of the wisdom of those who have shaped it in the crucible of experience and prayer.

The purpose of this book is to examine the ways the centrifugal waves of Luther's movement, and of the wider movements into which it fed, reached the shores of England, and to examine a few of the ways Reformation concerns and principles shook and shaped English life in the decades following their arrival. It does so through the lens of ten remarkable human beings, ten individual lives characterized by both strength and frailty and yet somehow transfigured by their encounter with what they felt the times demanded of them: of their intellects, commitments, public service, literary efforts, prayers and actions. Catholic and Protestant, women and men, rich and poor, they are icons of faithfulness. Their faithfulness was experienced and expressed in vastly different ways and towards wildly varied ends, but points to some common affirmations of what kind of virtues really ought to characterize a properly Christian, fully human, life. Between them, they tell one version of the story of the English Reformation; more importantly, they point to the beauty and the integrity of the living faith that resides beneath all their argument, disputation and polemic.

What is strange in that, however, is that none of those in this volume would have thought of themselves as Lutheran, except perhaps for Queen Elizabeth I, whose 'secret heart' in religious matters is notoriously tricky to read. For some, Luther's ideas were dangerous heresy, taking England out of the fold of Catholic Christianity and striking at the heart of practices and beliefs they considered essential for authenticity. For others, they didn't go far enough, fatally compromising with Catholicism when what was needed was a root-and-branch renewing of English Christian life. For yet others, the passage of time meant that Luther's ideas now seemed a distant and rather irrelevant set of propositions, not speaking to the demands and exigencies of their age. Geographical distance and a unique set of circumstances ensured that England's Reformation, when it came, was not solely or even primarily dependent on the work of this complex German monk. His influence was felt in some areas (the 'Matthew' Bible of 1537, which King Henry allowed to be published, included his famous preface to the letter to the Romans, for instance), but in general his distinctive version of 'Evangelical' – that is, gospel-derived – Christianity was disapproved of in the early English Reformation, seemed half-hearted to Protestants in the middle period, and had become largely the outmoded product of a distant era by the seventeenth century.

So why examine these lives at all, themselves perhaps rather distant, potentially irrelevant and certainly belonging to times and seasons vastly different from our own? It may seem strange to have to justify such an endeavour, but the novelist L. P. Hartley's assertion that 'the past is a foreign country: they do things differently there' seems now deeply and widely shared. And in a sense it is true, of course; but it is equally true that unless we also retain a biblical sense of 'the rock from which we were hewn', of the memory of who we are and how we come to be here, we shall remain infinitely impoverished by our amnesia as we seek faithful ways to live in this uniquely challenging age. Gordon Rupp himself, in making the case for what he called 'the enthralling dialogue between generations', cautioned against settling for the monologue that simply imposes our own concerns and questions on the past, the mistake Rowan Williams describes as regarding history as 'just the present in fancy dress'. Rupp likens the careful skills required in this dialogue to those required in brain surgery: good historians, he claims, 'really do call old worlds into being to redress the balance of the new'. They identify those questions pertinent to human experience in every time and place, and for the answering of which we need wisdom, resources, insights and energies beyond our own, and beyond even all those of the present age.[3]

In my own pondering of the purpose of history, I keep returning again and again to T. S. Eliot's elusive, mysterious and yet remarkable meditation on his visit to an English Reformation site, the village of Little Gidding, discussed in Chapter 9 of this book. Something struck him that day with great impact, concerning this 'dialogue between generations', and he laboured to convey it in poetry. In part, his epiphany was about the need for reverence: to honour, without fully understanding, past lives in their faithfulness and integrity, as well as in their inability to see as we do. As he put it:

> You are not here to verify,
> Instruct yourself, or inform curiosity
> Or carry report. You are here to kneel
> Where prayer has been valid.[4]

It is the aim of this book, in part, to allow us to honour the integrity of the women and men it portrays, people in whose lives prayer was 'valid', even as we cannot understand them or inhabit their ways of seeing and understanding the world.

But Eliot also invokes Rupp's sense of what is pertinent to every age and what connects those of every age, no matter how different the 'externals' of their context. He speaks of history as 'a pattern of timeless moments', and is moved to find himself caught up in one, an intersection of past and present in which he feels himself somehow able to communicate with those long dead, and in which too he senses the reconciliation only time can bring:

> We cannot revive old factions
> We cannot restore old policies
> Or follow an antique drum.
> These men, and those who opposed them
> And those whom they opposed
> Accept the constitution of silence
> And are folded in a single party.[5]

In seeking to be open to this moment, this meeting, this intersection, he mysteriously finds himself able to communicate with the past, and thus able better to understand its relationship to the present. He senses something of the life of God, in whom all things hold together and time itself is transfigured:

> And what the dead had no speech for, when living,
> They can tell you, being dead: the communication
> Of the dead is tongued with fire beyond the language of the
> living.[6]

Such 'timeless moments' cannot simply be manufactured. But as Eliot's language suggests, they can be sought in careful, prayer-like ways. We may look for similar portals in which the dead may speak to us only by first entering their world, with respect and caution and curiosity. What we hear there, from them, will be ours alone to hear: given to us in the communion of saints through the love and grace of the God who holds all people, living and departed, in one eternal embrace. So this book offers some tentative suggestions about what we may or may not find, as we kneel and listen. Above all it seeks to facilitate a conversation between the Reformation Church in England, with all its contentions and aspirations, and the modern Church, so desirous of new life, new hope and a fresh sense of its own connectedness to its mission. May the dialogue be rich and fruitful.

Jonathan Dean
Birmingham, Trinity Sunday 2017

Acknowledgements

Two of these reflections have had their provenance elsewhere. Chapter 2 is an expanded version of a sermon preached at Jesus College, Cambridge for their 'Reforming the Reformations' series in Spring 2017, and I wish to record my indebtedness to the Dean of Chapel, the Revd Paul Dominiak, for the great honour of preaching about Cranmer in his own college, and for the wonderful hospitality I received. Chapter 3 is based on a paper given at a Methodist Research Seminar held at Wesley House, Cambridge in April 2017. Without the gentle encouragement of the Revd Dr Cindy Wesley it would not have been written, and I'm thankful for her ministry.

Three fine historians of the Church have been in my mind as I wrote what follows. The book is in part a sort of affectionate homage to the late Revd Professor Gordon Rupp, a great Luther scholar and Methodist minister whose writings, 30 years after his death, remain a formidable, eloquent, witty and seminal contribution to Reformation studies and who, although I never met him, consistently informs and inspires me. It is modelled in particular, though obviously in a vastly inferior way, on his *Just Men* and *Six Makers of English Religion*, in drawing brief 'pen portraits' of those whose lives demand our attention and gratitude. Several of his books were given to me from the library of the late Revd Dr John Newton by his wife Rachel, just before he himself died, and are now cherished possessions. I am grateful for John's ministry and scholarship too, which has so shaped Methodism and the wider Church, fostering mutual understanding and wider ecumenical reconciliation. To their names I would add that of

Bishop Geoffrey Rowell, another fine historian of Anglicanism and my undergraduate chaplain and mentor. Geoffrey's influence in my own life has been of enormous importance. He died just as I completed the manuscript; his influence will be clear throughout. May they all, Gordon, John and Geoffrey, rest in peace and rise in glory.

I am grateful beyond words to my friends, who happen also to be my colleagues, at the Queen's Foundation in Birmingham. To live, move and have my being in a place of such faithfulness, scholarship and generosity is an enormous privilege. Andrew Hayes, Judith Rossall and Andrea Russell have made time to share illuminating conversations about the Reformation with me, and Mark Earey has done the same for particular chats about our beloved Thomas Cranmer. Dave Allen, Ashley Cocksworth, Jane Craske, Gary Hall, Jeanette Hartwell, Paul Nzacahayo, Katherine Onion, Fran Porter, Dulcie McKenzie, Kerry Scarlett, Helen Stanton, Richard Sudworth and Rachel Starr have graciously offered encouragement, support and good advice. Chapter 3 will reveal particular debts of insight I owe to Nicola Slee. David Hewlett, our Principal, is an unfailing source of wisdom, pastoral care and generosity. Michael Gale is the best theological librarian in the business. Eunice and John Attwood are at once perfect neighbours, generous friends and infinite sources of wisdom. For them all, I give heartfelt thanks.

My family is always owed thanks for their toleration and even encouragement of my obsessions. My partner Trey Hall especially is forced to endure living with the dead, and with my absences in the office, on a routine basis, and does so with extraordinary kindness and grace. I am so blessed by his unstinting support and enthusiasm, and his unfailing love and care.

The book is dedicated to two members of my extended family, Martin Forward and Udho Igwe. Their friendship, in good times and bad, has been a source of immense strength and incalculable consolation. Martin's scholarly interest in the Reformation has also been formative, and I remain grateful, now that we live far apart,

ACKNOWLEDGEMENTS

for memories of conversations about Bishop Longland, Anne Boleyn and George Herbert, among others. Our shared musical tastes form the background to the opening of Chapters 7 and 10. I am so grateful to them both, for their kindness, hospitality and love, through which my life has been immeasurably enriched. Udho died, after dealing graciously and courageously with a cruel disease, midway through the writing of this book. To her, and to Martin, it is offered, with my love. I share with Martin the confident hope that one day we shall all, in the words of Thomas More, merrily meet in heaven.

1

The Ground of Charity: Thomas More

He was the greatest Englishman of his age. He has a strong claim
to be the greatest of any age. In learning he was a polymath,
gifted in languages, fluent in philosophy, made curious by the
acquisition of knowledge in all its forms and genres. In literature
he was a fluent and poetic writer, capable of both exquisite,
captivating language and mordant, devastating polemic. He was
a lawyer of renown who rose to the top of his profession, insightful
in judgement, incisive in forensic evaluation of the case and
implacable in the prosecution of what he deemed dangerous to
the realm. His friendship was the most prized of his generation
and his company widely sought after. In the presence of Thomas
More the world seemed a better place: one of enjoyment, wit
and laughter. His circle counted themselves fortunate, and for a
while his circle included his king. Henry VIII adored him, quite
as susceptible to More's qualities and virtues as anyone else, and
preferred him to the highest office in the land below his own.
Then came one of history's most dramatic falls from grace, and a
traitor's ignominious death on Tower Hill. The flower of the age,
felled by the executioner's axe and the power of the state he had
himself until so recently commanded.

Five centuries after his death, Thomas More has continued to
interest and intrigue us. He has been co-opted into all manner of
causes and admired by all manner of enquirers. His portrayal in
literature has been bewilderingly dissonant, from Robert Bolt's
saintly champion of individual conscience in *A Man for all Seasons*
to Hilary Mantel's dour, ruthless heretic hunter in *Wolf Hall*. Both
are great works of literature; both fail egregiously in capturing

1

him cleanly and interpreting him accurately. But then he is hard to capture, a man whose parts and passions it is hard for us to put together in a way that makes sense. We are perhaps no more able than was his wife to understand why he might give his life to prevent a divorce; we are certainly unable to comprehend a man who would push so zealously for the execution of heretics. His practice of traditional methods of self-mortification, wearing a hair shirt as part of his personal spiritual discipline, seems to sit most uneasily for his modern assessors with his 'merry tales' and his abundance of good humour. It might even be hard to piece the constituent components of his life together and comprehend his sheer variety and dazzling brilliance, and the way the great causes of his life were, for him, all of a piece, demanding, when the ultimate test came, nothing less than everything.

The diverse causes of his life, too, have made him fair game for a whole gamut of those seeking to co-opt him into their own pantheon. Lenin saw in *Utopia*, More's tour de force of philosophical imagination, the ideas that laid the ground for Communism, and celebrated More on a public monument in Moscow accordingly. The victims of Soviet Communism instead saw More, and his *Utopia*, as an accurate predictor of the tendency of Communist nations towards servitude and the brutalization of their people. Some project on to him the very modern idea, wholly alien to him, of the absolute prerogative of individuals to live by their private convictions and personal beliefs. The Roman Catholic Church, naturally enough, has found the nature of his stance against the Reformation and his willingness to die for the primacy of the Pope a compelling exemplar of both piety and courage. We will have much more to say about the nature of his stand and the use made of it by the generation immediately following his own, but it is interesting to note for now that More's canonization came only in 1935, a helpful propaganda moment for Pius XI at a time of increased defensiveness at the Vatican. Nor did the proclamation of his sainthood particularly dwell on the agony by which he reached his *eventual* belief in papal authority.

Nevertheless, he is now the patron saint of both lawyers and politicians: many of the former would be aghast at many of More's legal methods; most of the latter would find his willingness to relinquish power because of principle entirely incomprehensible.

Perhaps the first key to thinking about Thomas More is to remember him as one of history's great 'bridges': born into one age and dying in the next, and finding the world dizzyingly changed in between. More entered the world at the very end of the medieval age (as we now think of things), into a well-to-do family in London, with Edward IV on the throne for the second time. He was just seven years old when the usurper Henry Tudor seized the crown, and the world as Englishmen had known it was thrown into chaos. More's family lost no time in accommodating themselves to the new order, however, and he was in effect apprenticed to the great bishop-cum-statesman of his own youth, John, Cardinal Morton, the Archbishop of Canterbury, who acted also as King Henry's Lord Chancellor. Young Thomas learned much as Morton's page that he would later remember and draw on when he inherited the lord chancellorship himself from another ecclesiastical politician, Thomas Wolsey. This early formation led to an Oxford education and then to the Inns of Court. The young lawyer, steeped in the religious commitments of his time and deeply invested in the 'new' learning with all its seemingly limitless potential, was on his way.

He also made the most important friendship of his life, even as he stood on the edge of a promising career. Desiderius Erasmus was in England in the late 1490s, near the beginning of his one-man effort to have all Europe adoringly at his feet. Erasmus embodied the kind of learning that was now the trend and that More was himself devouring, and the two of them, both just beginning to make a way in the world that would make them famous for centuries to come, soon fell heavily for one another, delighting in all they shared and in the rare company of an intellectual equal. They also shared a keen eye for the flaws and foibles of their fellow humanity, a biting wit in which to frame them and a devastating turn of phrase with which to describe them. With the future constraints of high office far ahead of him too, More was more free to pursue his philosophical interests wherever they led him, in the company of his beloved Erasmus who, eight years his senior, may also have acted as older brother and mentor, at least for a while.

The ancient languages and cultures of the Greek and Roman worlds, and the firm belief that their rediscovery contained the intellectual and cultural power to revivify European life and thought, formed the heart of the 'new' approach to learning that More and his new best friend shared and came to exemplify. Erasmus in particular also came to the view that there should be a particular focus in this on the ancient and authoritative texts of Christianity: if they could be rediscovered, reassimilated and re-presented to the Church and its people, nothing less than the renewal of the faith itself would then follow. Supremely, Erasmus later laboured to retranslate the Bible itself, from the thousand-year-old Vulgate of Jerome into a new Latin version, more accurate, lively and better framed for the needs of a new age. It was an ambitious, exciting, all-consuming project – new methods for a renewed Church in a changed world – and Erasmus was its intellectual leader, its guiding spirit and its ablest scholar. He came to England at the beginning of a career that was to encompass and inform the life of a whole continent. Like More, he always remained both adamant that his discoveries were mandating radical reform for the Church, and yet also viscerally devoted to its unity of belief, devotion and common life all across the known world.

It surprises some to learn of the extent to which, in these early years of their friendship, More and Erasmus criticized their Church and those who led it. Indeed, to some they appear proto-Protestants. A decade and more ahead of Martin Luther's fateful decision to challenge Catholicism's teaching on penitence and the afterlife, the two friends were calling for the kinds of reform later to be common parlance from the 'Evangelicals' across Europe.

They were advocates of a Bible in English, properly translated to avoid error but enabling literate people better to mine the riches of their own Scriptures. They found the proliferation of myriad monastic orders in Europe, all with their own peculiar and particular rules and customs, traditions and doctrines, a monstrous waste of money and a massive distraction from the essential task of deepening lay piety. They were aghast at the follies and extravagances of some elements of Catholic devotion: the excessive toiling to spurious pilgrimage sites to venerate alleged bits of saintly bone or scraps of apostolic tunics, not to mention the obviously erroneous claims of many churches to possess fragments of the true cross or sightings of the Virgin. In their mind, well-intentioned Christians were failing to give attention to what might actually aid their spiritual growth, while being fleeced by the con men and women of the medieval veneration business.

More had in fact pondered a monastic vocation early in his life, before deciding, with characteristically clear self-knowledge, that it would not be for him. As a family man, lawyer and statesman, he did always seek to enshrine a monastic mode into his daily rhythm of life, in prayer, devotion, learning and solitude. But for a mix of reasons likely to be far more complex than we have sometimes assumed (it wasn't all about a resistance to celibacy!), he freighted the balance of his life in favour of family while retaining a monk-like cell in the grounds of his Chelsea home. Erasmus, by contrast, was a monk: of a sort. He had gained a measure of release from his Augustinian vows to become a freelance scholar, and his commitment to his own order waned with the years. And it was a book containing an excoriating attack on monks and monasticism that was also his most public tribute to More and their friendship. The *Praise of Folly* (in Latin, *Encomium Moriae*) of 1511 contained in its very title the pun that revealed its dedicatee. A great lampoon of the idiocies and excesses of the age, combined with a heartfelt call for renewed simplicity in the Church's life, it provoked admiration, hilarity and scorn in almost equal measure. As satire it remains among the liveliest and most effective examples of the genre. But it set an example, too, in elegance, fluency and wit, which More's own greatest work was to mirror and recall.

Erasmus was the prime mover in ensuring the publication of More's *Utopia* in 1516. It has never ceased to fascinate, amuse, amaze and above all cause consternation, wherever it has been read in the five hundred years since. An early literary marvel of the modern age, and still one of the finest books ever written by an Englishman, it is an impressionistic work of great genius, teasing and toying with its readers. In the light of More's later career, and of his obdurate refusal to tolerate heretics or countenance the royal divorce, the playful spirit of *Utopia* can seem puzzling. More holds ideas up to the light, tests theories and advances strange notions, all in the cause of an examination of good governance and the wisest way to order human affairs.

The mysterious traveller, Raphael Hythlodaeus, whom More creates as his dialogue partner in *Utopia*, recounts his experience of studying the island of Utopia, founded by Utopus, over the course of five years. Society is ordered rather differently there: princes are elected; there is no private property; priests may marry and divorce; euthanasia is permitted; wealth and material goods are scorned (slaves' chains and chamber pots are made of gold to encourage this). Perhaps most strikingly, couples intending to marry are required to see one another naked before the marriage as a way of helping to ensure compatibility. Clearly, there are elements of Utopian life the mature More would have found horrifying if enacted in early sixteenth-century England, but that is to miss the point of this extraordinary exercise in philosophical imagination, which was itself fashioned after the great dialogues of the ancient world, most notably those of Plato. *Utopia* was meant to provoke conversation, to engage readers' minds and stimulate reflection on human affairs. To read it as a literal blueprint for an actual system of governance denies its power. Like the philosophical equivalent of a painting by Salvador Dali, it sought to reflect reality by playing with it, asking its readers to be delighted and bewildered by this evocation of a strange and remote country such that they returned to their own with fresh questions and different eyes.

The religious polity of the Utopians has seemed especially puzzling to some readers, given More's own commitments and later reputation. King Utopus, seeing the capacity of religions to be a source of friction and division within countries like his:

> made a decree, that it should be lawful for every man to favour and follow what religion he would, and that he might do the best he could to bring others to his opinion, so that he did it peaceably, gently, quietly and soberly, without hasty and contentious rebuking and inveighing against others. If he could not by fair and gentle speech induce them unto his opinion, yet he should use no kind of violence, and refrain from displeasant and seditious words . . . This law did King Utopus make not only for the maintenance of peace . . . but also because he thought this decree should make for the furtherance of religion.[7]

Here again, however, More's imaginative playfulness toys with us, imagining the enlightened condition of a nation that does not know the unifying Truth of Christianity, and contrasting the natural attitude of such a nation with the petty and sometimes destructive squabbles of humanity more generally. Nor, in his mind, would the behaviour of the Reformers have kept to the legal boundaries the King had himself imposed.

In any case, *Utopia* only heightened More's renown. The book had been conceived and written while on diplomatic missions in Europe, and his success in them guaranteed he would continue to rise in the affairs of the government. He became Speaker of the Commons in 1523 and Chancellor of the Duchy of Lancaster two years later. The King adored him and sought his company frequently, but apparently not in a way More ever entirely trusted, if at all. More's son-in-law and biographer, William Roper, once commented to his father-in-law on the familiarity and warm jocularity with which Henry treated him on his visits to the More family home in Chelsea. More replied that he did indeed feel fortunate to be the King's favourite, but that such intimacy with monarchs was often a dangerous thing: 'for if my head could win him a castle in France, it would not fail to go'. Prescience and insight like that, as we will see, were among More's greatest virtues.

The closeness of his family life was the bedrock of everything else, and the hinterland of his public life and rapid promotion to the high offices of state. More had married Jane, who died after bearing four children. Having chosen marriage over the cloister, More moved with extraordinary and even mildly scandalous speed to remarry, choosing Alice Middleton, a wealthy widow whose strength of character and force of opinion he sometimes mocked but whose presence he certainly relied on with a young family and many and growing responsibilities. Against expectation and received opinion, More insisted on educating his daughters as highly as his sons; indeed, his daughter Margaret was one of the cleverest and most accomplished women of her age, as well as her father's counsellor and closest companion. Theirs was a remarkable relationship of confidence, mutual affection and regard, and for both it was a vital one, both in times of prosperity and amid the seasons of crisis and insecurity that followed.

It's at this stage of More's life, and in the legal career that led to it, that we encounter one of the most difficult elements of his character for modern people: his resistance to heresy. Thomas More pursued those who propagated heretical opinions with a ferocity and a ruthlessness we find unconscionable and that many have judged cruel. How could such a champion of the 'new' learning, such a doyen of the European intelligentsia, have countenanced such behaviour, which involved ensuring that those whose religious beliefs did not represent orthodox Roman Catholicism were burned at the stake and thus absolutely obliterated from the earth, along with their views? And why, as lawyer, public official and ultimately a statesman, did he make the fight against heresy such a central and unrelenting emphasis in his career, on behalf of his nation?

To begin to understand we must do More the courtesy of remembering that he was a child of his time. It is almost impossible for us to imagine a world that knew the level of religious unity More was born into, and it is an even further reach to appreciate the gratitude More and his generation experienced for the security and unanimity this produced in their life. Despite the usual human disagreements about various other matters, the fabric of European society was knit together by a shared view of divine presence and of the ways human beings might order their lives around that central conviction. The papacy represented all that bound Christendom together in charity and kinship, not merely a symbol but also the guarantor of community. To see the need for reform by no means undermined the comfort and pride to be taken from belonging to this extraordinary society, whose authority was vested in an institution that stretched back to Christ himself and the primacy of St Peter, and whose appeal was thus rooted in the strongest claims to respect and admiration. To be a Christian in More's day was far from a simple private conviction about spiritual matters, or a personal choice to accept a particular understanding of life and death; it was an acknowledgement of one's membership in and debt to a vast community of others, our brothers and sisters in faith and in life itself, stretching through time and space, which anchored life in the present more firmly and more meaningfully than was possible easily to convey. Membership of the Church was one's birthright and one's privilege, bringing with it the stable ordering of society itself, not only in the particular country one lived in but across the Christian world.

For Thomas More, an attack on this vision of unity was an attack on humanity itself and on the providence of the God in whose wisdom the world had been ordered this way. It was to put at risk not only a particular religious view of certain matters but the very way of life of all Christendom. To be a heretic was not merely to hold views incompatible with the Church's theology but to be an anarchist. It was to mount an attack on the safety of the realm and the security of the whole people. Like a cancer, More believed, heresy voraciously devoured everything it touched, laid waste to every element of common life and destroyed the welfare of everyone it reached. Far better to eradicate its proponents absolutely than to allow its toxic effects to spread through the Christian world like some ravening parasite. The merest tolerance of it would soon prove a fatal error, he believed.

More felt that his view of heresy was proven, too, in the words and actions of a German monk, Martin Luther, and in the dangerous protection granted him by his prince. King Henry, at that point eager to impress the Pope with his loyalty, had attacked Luther's theology in 1521 in print, a work that won him papal gratitude and a papal title, ironically carried by all his successors up to the present: Defender of the Faith. Luther, never one to enjoy criticism, fought back savagely and was in turn rebutted by the King's good servant, Thomas More. His *Response to Luther* is vitriolic and scatological in tone: most unsaintlike, except for the fact that it takes its cue from Luther's own language and abusive rhetoric. More followed up his published work on heresy in 1528 with the *Dialogue Concerning Heresies*, a work that made the point that Luther's views, left unchecked, had indeed swiftly turned to chaos in Germany, with the Peasants' Revolt of 1525. The widening chasm between Luther and More, both of whom saw the need for reform in the Church's affairs, was the central and crucial difference between them on the authority of the Church and the Pope. More saw the papacy, with all its flaws, as the guarantor of connection to the Church in every other place and time. Luther came to see the papacy as Antichrist, a perversion of the gospel, whose place in European life was a scandal. There could be no compromise between them.

So More the wit and teller of merry tales was no more incompatible with More the hunter of heretics than is a contemporary humorist with someone who espouses the eradication of groups like ISIS. Even witty people might think that existential threats to humanity should be overcome, and we need to think of the heresy of More's day as something rather akin to that – at least in his mind – to realize that his hatred of it did not stem from cruelty but from his own humanity and his growing duty as a statesman to guarantee the safety of his land and its citizens. In dealing with heretics More could be patient, compassionate and persistent, at least until they proved themselves obdurate or unrelenting. Indeed, his own beloved daughter, Margaret, married a man, the William Roper we just met, who underwent a dalliance with heresy. It wasn't an easy time in the More household, but More acted towards his wayward son-in-law with restraint and yet with commitment, willing him to return to the fold of the Church, which, in time, he did.

This commitment to the extirpation of heresy in England thus became central in More's increasingly illustrious public career, but it was a deeply personal cause as well. Late into the night, in his study in Chelsea, he continued to write lengthy, detailed, colourful treatises against its ideas and warning of its baleful influence. Simply, he believed nothing so absolutely vital to England's future prosperity and security. When, in 1529, Simon Fish published a brief pamphlet called *The Supplication of the Beggars*, which criticized the faults of the clergy and argued for some of the emerging tenets of the Protestant Reformation, More's response, the *Supplication of Souls*, was many times longer and infinitely more detailed and verbose. He refused to see in the men who conveyed God's very life to the mass of ordinary people the kinds of blackguards and crooks Fish asserted them to be, and in any case insisted on the ancient view that even sinful priests still validly offered the sacraments to the faithful. When William Tyndale challenged the *Dialogue Concerning Heresies*, his work was met with an even more massive one, the *Confutation of Tyndale's Answer*. The quality is perhaps less impressive than the width at this point, as More insists on dealing with every point made by Tyndale with almost wearying detail and often aggressive vigour. But by this time More's public life was ending abruptly, and he faced a different kind of threat altogether: the anger of his king.

Thomas More had never been a supporter of the King's plan to divorce Queen Katherine. While doing his best to remain a good and faithful servant of his monarch, he had always offered clear private counsel to Henry that the marriage was legal and that there were no good grounds, legally, morally or religiously, to end it. His appointment to the Lord Chancellor's office was made despite Henry's knowledge of this, and on the assurance that More would not have to prosecute the matter in a way that conflicted with his conscience. The technical questions involved in the King's 'Great Matter' were certainly complex, but for More there was one central and reliable aspect to it: the marriage had been formed after a clear and specific papal dispensation had been issued that dismissed any potential obstacles arising from Katherine's first marriage to Prince Arthur. Katherine's fervent assertions that that marriage had been unconsummated should also, in any case, be respected and believed, More held. So he saw no grounds for divorce, despite the lack of a male heir, and he saw no way that canvassing other individuals, organizations and universities for approval of the matter constituted anything other than disrespect and divisiveness at the national level and the appalling public humiliation of a good and faithful Christian woman at a more personal one. This was all bad enough, therefore; much worse was to come.

With increasing frustration, Henry went so far as to assert his headship of the English Church and deny the supremacy of the Pope in religious matters. Religious life in England could carry on as before, he assured, but with himself as its ultimate arbiter, the lord of the spiritual elements of his people's lives as much as he was of the political, social and economic ones. And conveniently, he could dispense in the matter of his own divorce and put right the injustice done to him by successive popes. This was not all purely cynical and manipulative on his part or that of his counsellors, as we will examine in more depth later. But as Henry moved in this direction he began to espouse views that to More were pure poison, the kind of heresy described above, wrong for all the reasons previously described. Henry, in his Lord Chancellor's mind, was seeking to sunder England absolutely from the common life of Christendom, from the shared patterns of devotion, obedience and mutuality of Europe and even from the Body of Christ itself; and all for a divorce that was unethical, cruel and unnecessary. All around him, previously conservative colleagues found ways to accommodate themselves to the clear shift about to take place, embracing the idea of the new 'royal supremacy' with apparent ease: Stephen Gardiner, the crafty Bishop of Winchester whom we'll meet again later, even went so far as to write a book, *On True Obedience*, publicly to flaunt his continued loyalty to Henry, despite his religious conservatism. Whatever Gardiner's true motives, it was a book he was later bitterly to regret; for More, it was one among many devastating indications that he was almost utterly alone in resisting the King's religious policy. Behind Gardiner and his ilk, those with tendencies towards the new 'evangelical' emphases relished the moment. Led by the King's sweetheart, Anne Boleyn, they prepared for their moment.

It was indeed the relish of such people, Cromwell and Cranmer foremost among them, that gave More particular anxiety and grievous concern. For all the King's assertions and assurances that nothing would change in the religious practices of the Church in England, that devotion and liturgy would carry on exactly as they had been under the oversight of Rome, More knew that the pressure from within the court, and through Anne and her party in particular, would be irresistible, and that there would be no means to prevent their influence. There was no way, he believed, the royal supremacy could represent anything other than England's descent into isolation, heresy and the risk of invasion and war. Above all, he simply did not believe that the papal supremacy could be cast off without rendering the English Church apostate, and he was unable to support the gradual legislative moves Henry was making towards such an outcome. And so he had no choice but to resign, something he did with great sorrow but also, it would seem, gratitude that he could retreat to his hinterland of family, literature and prayer, to a life of private devotion and public silence, his career in politics over. That, at any rate, was the deal he thought he had struck with his monarch.

Henry had been ruthless with Cardinal Wolsey when he had failed to bring about the divorce, but Wolsey had at least agreed with him. In the face of More's disagreement and deliberate refusal to bow to his wishes, something even darker and more unpleasant, a side of his character to become increasingly prevalent later in his reign, emerged. It corroded the King's soul like acid that More, the great thinker, lawyer and statesman of the realm, was known to resist him and flout his authority. More kept his word, retreating to Chelsea in silence and refusing to offer any criticism, private or public, of the divorce or the King; but it wasn't enough for Henry's unrelenting narcissism to be resisted in this way. Further, although More acknowledged Parliament's right to proclaim Anne Boleyn the new Queen, he refused to attend her coronation in 1533, claiming ill health. The circle began to close around him. Cromwell and others instituted efforts to accuse him of corruption or embroil him in treason or scandal. These were unsuccessful but were a clear indication that he could not escape for long. His dream of a quiet, unmolested retirement in the bosom of his family was never going to be realized.

The final reckoning came in 1534 when Henry, presumably with More at the forefront of his mind, instituted an oath of acceptance to the new Act of Succession, which could be demanded of any subject and included an acknowledgement of the royal supremacy. Entirely predictably, More was soon asked to subscribe, and taken to Lambeth Palace for the process, rowed downriver on a bright spring day. Given time to ponder his refusal to sign, he observed the evident joy of those, such as Cromwell and Cranmer, whose moment of influence had now come, as they organized the oath-taking and delightedly took counsel with one another in the sunshine. Under mounting pressure and in unimaginable mental torment, More refused; even though he was willing to allow Parliament's right to decide the succession, this was not enough to satisfy the King's absolute need to be approved, submitted to and obeyed. Consequently, Sir Thomas was imprisoned in the Tower. He was never to leave, until taken for trial and subsequently execution.

We owe to this last, traumatic, testing phase of More's life some of his deepest wisdom and most lasting literary work. Facing the ultimate winnowing down of his life, to what really lent it meaning and value, he searched his soul and brought his formidable gifts of mind and heart to bear on the quest for purpose. Sometimes those who describe this period perhaps make it rather too easy: More certainly prayed hard and often during his imprisonment, but we should not romantically see this time as the eventual realization of the monastic life that had so intrigued him in his youth. He was utterly alone: separated from the family life that gave him strength and security; increasingly deprived of the books that fired his imagination and connected him to the world he loved; abandoned by former friends who now found his association toxic and career-damaging; and facing the certainty of a rigged trial, public humiliation and terrible execution. And yet through opening this agony and isolation up in prayer and honest self-reflection, he did find it shot through with the possibility of hope and even redemption. The promise of heaven became more than a pious afterthought; humanity's essential oneness with the divine assumed greater power and meaning for him and he was somehow able to assign a new sense of value to many of the things he had formerly chased, realizing their ultimate vanity and futility.

Being Thomas More, of course, he wrote about the consequences of such spiritual reflection for as long as he was allowed the means to do so. The *Dialogue of Comfort Against Tribulation* reveals him back to his literary best, a book of merry tales, witty insights and warm humanity that nevertheless makes some very serious points along the way. With poignancy and humour he explores the contours of the human spirit in times of adversity, peril and isolation, and the nature of the comfort to be found by Christians who discover, underneath all their earthly trials, the everlasting arms of God's mercy, grace and eternal keeping. In his final unfinished book, *On the Sadness of Christ*, More sought to remind himself, perhaps even before his readers, of Christianity's great, central, unique promise: a God who takes flesh, treads the path of loss, suffering and sorrow and thus is able truly to claim to be 'with' a wounded humanity in ways that transform the human condition. If theological reflection of this kind had always been central to his way of life, it now assumed an even greater urgency and power.

These latter days also produced some of the most heartbreaking and yet inspiring correspondence ever written, as More communicated to and through his daughter Margaret, his intellectual companion and emotional support. His honesty with her is touching, but through his grief and sadness shine also hope and acceptance. In the intensely personal devotional writings of this period, too, we see the man's true soul, pared down now to its essence, shorn of worldly authority and status but reflecting a forgiving spirit that had always been there and always been central, whatever his critics suggest. The *Godly Instruction on How to Treat Those Who Wrong Us* of 1534 might stand for so much of his writing at this time, with its stress on the reconciling grace of God, operative especially powerfully when the trials of this life are past:

> Bear no malice nor evil to no man living. For either the man is good or naught. If he be good, and I hate him, then am I naught. If he be naught, either he shall amend and die good, and go to God: or abide naught, and die naught and go to the Devil. And then let me remember, that if he shall be saved, he shall not fail (if I be saved too, as I trust to be) to love me very heartily, and I shall then in likewise love him. And why should

I now then, hate one for this while, which shall hereafter love me for evermore, and why should I be now then enemy to him, with whom I shall in time coming, be coupled in eternal friendship? . . . But let us that are no better than men of a mean sort, ever pray for such merciful amendment in other folk, as our own conscience showeth us that we have need in ourself.[8]

At his trial, despite the privations of his situation, his absolute isolation and the enormous strain he must have been under, More made a magnificent effort in the face of great difficulties to defend himself, asserting his right to be silent, without that silence implying guilt, his unimpeachable conduct and service to the realm and the unprecedented nature of the events then engulfing the nation. Although he had the right of things and the unanswerable case, of course, his true opinions were well and widely known, and he had no chance of escaping the wrath of a king who felt betrayed. In the end it was assuredly a perjury that convicted him, when Richard Rich, one of More's interrogators, claimed that More had, in an unguarded moment, revealed his true heart on the matter of the King's claimed religious supremacy. As More himself was quick to point out, having so carefully avoided incriminating himself over so many years, in conversation with friends, family, statesmen and expert lawyers, he would hardly have betrayed himself to a jumped-up parvenu like Rich in an obviously contrived situation. Nevertheless, Rich was believed by a jury with no option but to convict. More was executed five days later, on 6 July 1535. As he himself said on the scaffold, he died as he had lived, 'the King's good servant: but God's first'.

Margaret Roper managed to save her father's severed head, after it had been publicly displayed as humiliation and warning for his 'treachery', and is believed to have buried it at St Dunstan's Church in Canterbury. His headless corpse was interred in the unmarked grave at St Peter ad Vincula Church in the Tower, where ironically it was joined by that of Queen Anne Boleyn less than a year later.

There is no more powerful witness to the pathological cruelty of Henry VIII than the shared grave of the man who died to save England's unity with Rome and the woman whose marriage to him ended it. Both alike were ruthlessly killed as traitors. Margaret also strove to publish her father's complete works, something only achieved over a decade after her death, in 1557, through the good offices of William Rastell. There needed to be no fears, however, about More's influence and lasting renown. In Chapter 5 we will see his pivotal importance to subsequent generations of English Catholics during the Reformation. Far beyond that, however, centuries after his life and death, he still embodies some of the best qualities and virtues of humane learning and living: wit, self-deprecating humour, humility and courage, grace under pressure and loyalty to the causes of his life. If some of those causes now seem to us quaint, outmoded or even cruel, they should not distract us from his extraordinary genius. No one has ever paid him tribute better or more memorably than Robert Whittington, in his *Vulgaria* of 1520:

> A man of an angel's wit and singular learning. I know not his fellow. For where is the man of that gentleness, lowliness and affability? And, as time requireth, a man of marvellous mirth and pastimes, and sometime of as sad gravity.
>
> A man for all seasons.

2

Ambition and Fidelity: Thomas Cranmer

Nowadays the little hamlet of Aslockton, in Nottinghamshire, lies just off the busy A52, connecting the north–south artery of the A1 with the urban sprawl of Nottingham and Derby. Nobody much therefore stops to notice it on their journey. Blink, and you miss it. It defines unprepossessing. In 1489 it didn't even have its own church; Thomas and Agnes Cranmer would have had to plough through the mud of the surrounding farmlands for the infant Thomas Junior to be baptized at Whatton. So you'd be forgiven for thinking that this lad, with such humble beginnings, must have been fired by great personal ambition to show the folks back home what was possible for someone like him: becoming a Doctor of Divinity and fellow (probably[9]) of Jesus College, Cambridge; a senior Counsellor to King Henry VIII; an ambassador to European courts; and ultimately sixty-ninth Archbishop of Canterbury and Primate of All England. If you add to that the fact that John Foxe, in his *Acts and Monuments* of 1563, has made him just about the most celebrated Protestant martyr ever, his record only increases.

But despite his great personal achievements, Cranmer wasn't really *personally* ambitious at all. He seems rather to have enjoyed his secluded life of scholarship and teaching in Cambridge and his circle of friends and colleagues there. Good humanist that he was, he loved the life of the mind: decades later, as Archbishop, he was still evidently drawing on the learning of his early life in his theological and liturgical projects, seeking to root his reforms of England's Church in the wider history of Christianity. Most fascinatingly of all, Cranmer's commitment to the companionship and intimacy of marriage was something absolutely impossible for a priest wanting to play any role on the national stage, at a time when marriage was forbidden to them. We are thus right to note that his second marriage in particular, contracted when he was ordained, clearly marks him out as someone affected by the new teaching that had taken root in Cambridge. But more than that, it would seem also to suggest that he had no desire or intention whatever to move beyond the relatively safe and cloistered confines of Cambridge, still less into the arena of national politics.

We can only surmise and imagine the agony of Cranmer's first marriage, to Joan. Later in his life, when it was used against him by his opponents seeking to exercise maximum leverage against him, he refused to be drawn on it. Joan died giving birth to their child, who did not survive either. The experience perhaps softened his own heart towards a king who wanted nothing more than a live male heir, having lost several in childbirth or through miscarriage. In any case, it was a time of searing loss, which he later, uniquely, took with him to the highest ecclesiastical office in the land. By that time he had married again, to Margarete, the niece of a continental reformer he had met while on the King's business abroad.

It was the pursuance of that business that also brought him, unexpectedly and to his own great shock, to Lambeth Palace, and tore him from the academic life that had both nurtured and protected his nascent Evangelical convictions. The particular business at hand, of course, was Henry VIII's 'Great Matter'. Unlike Sir Thomas More, Cranmer was willing wholeheartedly to help the King in his quest for a divorce. His suggestion that an old precedent be tried in this case too was seized on by Cardinal Thomas Wolsey, who then sent the Cambridge don in pursuit of his own good idea. Put simply, Cranmer's advice was that the European universities be consulted on the divorce, in the hope that the English authorities might pile up a great weight of incontrovertible opinions from academics and scholars all across the continent. Even the Pope would have to give way in the face of such overwhelming – and such impressively intellectual – evidence. As he pursued his case, Cranmer simultaneously made some friends and continued to nurture his views. As he went about it, Archbishop William Warham died. And the King was so impressed with his new ambassador, this intellectual with an eye for a plan and a desire to advance his monarch's interests, that he knew exactly who should bring those skills, and that intent, to the throne of St Augustine.

Cranmer's promotion to the See of Canterbury therefore came as a meteoric and rather unexpected one, and was as much the result of political shenanigans as of his own talents, which had yet to be proved in the holding of high ecclesiastical office, still less his own burning ambition. He was no Thomas Wolsey. And when Henry's chief enforcer in religious as in all other matters, Thomas Cromwell, muscled in on Cranmer's jurisdiction and authority, as a layman, the Archbishop seems genuinely not to have minded a whit, as his estates were given away and his powers curtailed. As he said himself:

> For I pray God never be merciful unto me at the general judgement, if I perceive in my heart that I set more by any title, name, or style that I write, than I do by the paring of an apple, farther than it shall be to the setting forth of God's word and will.[10]

Making a difference in the lives and faith of the English people was what fired him, as well as the absolute imperative of loyalty to the King. And here we must pause a moment and seek to understand the extraordinary motivation behind that unswerving fidelity to a man who had just turned the realm upside down to divorce a queen.

If some of Sir Thomas More's views, on heresy and how to deal with it, or the essential unity of Christendom, seem impossibly strange and old-fashioned to us today, and are used occasionally as cudgels to beat him with, we ought to remember that Thomas Cranmer's whole career, his entire life of reform, church governance, liturgical innovation and royal service, rested on an equally strange premise, for which he is rarely questioned. He was a staunch believer in what became known as the royal supremacy: Henry's 'realization' that, in ceding authority to the Pope in the affairs of the English Church, he was actually, negligently and culpably, giving away authority that was his, from God. Slowly, those around the King all came to share this view, with varying levels of genuine conviction and personal integrity. For Cranmer, it was an absolute article of faith. Henry Tudor, he firmly believed, was just as much the head of the English Church as he was of the English judiciary, the English army or indeed of any other part of the nation's life. These were his prerogatives by birth and by divine right, as monarch. They could not be given away and they had to be upheld; indeed, they brought a huge and solemn responsibility upon any King to ensure that the Church was reformed, efficient, scripturally ordered and, above all, faithfully inculcating the Christian faith in the hearts and minds of the people.

It was a belief, too, from which Cranmer never wavered, except for a brief moment at the tortured end of his life. When 'fair weather' royal supremacists, men like Bishop Stephen Gardiner who had actually written a whole book *On the True Obedience* to show Henry his loyalty, fell away on the accession of Mary in order to revert to papal obedience, Cranmer could not. Even though Mary's religion dismayed and appalled him, he believed that she was God's anointed and deeply regretted his own small part in the efforts to subvert the succession in favour of Jane Grey. At his trial he was even manipulated into agreeing that, when Emperor, Nero had been the head of the Church. A 'gotcha' moment indeed, but evidence of his absolute and unswerving commitment to the idea.

Cranmer's ambition, then, although it was fierce, lay in his twin guiding commitments, the two great causes of his life: absolute obedience to the King as God's anointed instrument, and the establishment of reformed, Evangelical Christianity in

England. Let us be careful, too, of the resonances those words have nowadays. What they meant for Cranmer were: a return to the Bible as the word of God, and which must therefore be available to people in the languages they spoke, to guide their believing and govern their living; a renewing of public worship so that the Bible was prominent and the central tenets of Christianity, shorn of what he saw as the excesses of medieval Catholicism, were plainly set forth; and a restoration of discipline, simplicity and piety in the lives of English men and women, that the kingdom might prosper under God. These were the objects of his ambition; and he set little store by *personal* advancement or diminishment, as long as he was able to see these causes triumph.

And triumph they did, during his time as Archbishop and largely through his leadership. The life of anyone serving at the court of Henry VIII was often fraught, dangerous and difficult, as we have seen. It was no different for Cranmer. The King's councillors were often bitterly divided among themselves about the course of religious change, and Cranmer's alliances with Queen Anne Boleyn and Thomas Cromwell clearly marked him out as an Evangelical with hopes for further and deeper progress. Nevertheless, even in this contested and sometimes frenzied atmosphere he made moves towards the creation of an English liturgy and the removal from the fabric and the worship of the English churches of those things that most smacked to him of the 'superstition' of medieval Catholicism. If the King's own commitment to the Mass was unmovable, he was persuadable in other areas of reform. Although the planning and execution of the most monumental of these changes, the dissolution of England's monasteries, was almost entirely Cromwell's work, Cranmer's efforts to oversee diocesan visitations and purge other remaining Catholic elements were unrelenting. And he succeeded in slowly shifting the King's own theology towards what Cranmer, like Luther, was coming to see as the central biblical truth of justification by faith alone, through the grace of God.

The proudest of all his achievements under Henry was the

publication of the 'Great' English Bible in 1540, the result of long and patient work with the King and somewhat against the grain of his preferences. It marked a moment of real shift towards reform, the Scriptures now available in every church and in the native language. Writing the preface to this epochal publishing event, the Archbishop was unrestrained in his enthusiasm for its moment and its possibility:

> Every man that cometh to the reading of this holy book ought to bring with him first and foremost this fear of Almighty God; and then next, a firm and stable purpose to reform his own self according thereunto; and so to continue, proceed and prosper from time to time, shewing himself to be a sober and fruitful hearer and learner. Which if he do, he shall prove at length well able to teach, though not with his mouth, yet with his living and good example; which is sure the most lively and effectuous form and manner of teaching.[11]

Writing to Cromwell he was if anything even more exuberant, thanking him for his support and championing of the Bible and promising him that, because of it, he would have 'a perpetual laud and memory of all them that be now, or hereafter shall be God's faithful people, and the favourers of his word'.[12]

Life for Cranmer after Cromwell's downfall, right after the Great Bible's publication, became lonelier and more dangerous. He was left to fight, often almost alone, for the continuation of the causes they had begun together. His enemies sought to destroy him and his reforming agenda: in 1543, Gardiner almost succeeded in persuading the King of Cranmer's heresy and duplicity. He was saved only because of something Cromwell himself had once pointed out: Henry loved his Archbishop with a tenderness and a genuine and unswerving fidelity that perhaps none other of his courtiers and counsellors ever enjoyed. We can only speculate as to why: apart from Cranmer's sterling work in the 'Great Matter', maybe there was something in the genuine goodness of the man that was able to penetrate even the sclerotic heart of the King. In any case, it was Cranmer for whom Henry called in his last illness, and who, holding the King's hand, offered prayers as he died.

Under Henry's young son, King Edward VI, Cranmer's ambition, as we have defined it, was allowed full reign. In these short six years, at the height of his powers, he revolutionized the Church in England. Subsequent generations have often forgotten the radicalism and breathtaking pace of the Edwardian years. But by the end of them, England stood poised to become the standard-bearer and leading theological powerhouse of Reformed Christian Europe. Setbacks at the hands of Catholic armies had left the great centres of the Protestant Reformation weakened and vulnerable, and even restored Catholicism to some of them. Cranmer established England in these difficult days for European Protestantism as the great hope for the ongoing cause of Evangelical Christianity. Amid a general welcome for refugees, Martin Bucer, Cranmer's great mentor and correspondent, came from Strasbourg and took up the Regius Professorship in the University of Cambridge. Peter Martyr Vermigli, the Italian-born reformer and lecturer in Strasburg, came over to the equivalent position in Oxford. Cranmer was planning a new great Ecumenical Council in England that would establish it as the bastion of Protestantism, the bulwark of Reformed Christianity throughout Europe. It was a remarkable vision and, because of his own efforts, an entirely attainable one.

There was also the matter of the liturgy of the English Church in these years. In his passion to bring the Church together in a shared pattern of worship that would instil Protestant emphases and beliefs into the faithful, Cranmer began an ambitious new liturgical project that culminated in two Books of Common Prayer in three years. The 1552 version, by now pared of almost all influences he deemed too close to superstition, encapsulated a wholesale revolution in the language of public worship. If today many people regard the BCP as the gold standard, whose language must remain unaltered and whose theology is classic middle-of-the-road Anglicanism, they forget the sheer reforming zeal of that 1552 edition, with its radical Eucharistic theology and its complete rejection of the medieval past and of its Church. Cranmer has influenced the language of worship in a way that actually gives him a claim to be the most successful of all the reformers – no one much beyond academic historians reads Luther's treatises or Calvin's *Institutes* these days, but almost everyone knows the cadences of Cranmer's prose and the beauty of his liturgy. But for all that, it entirely misunderstands Cranmer's own ambition not to see that he would never have regarded the BCP as a finished work, frozen in time. It was a work in progress, to be refined and reformed itself in order to continue making the truths of Christianity accessible to the ordinary Christians he cared so passionately about.

Cranmer had stood in Westminster Abbey at Edward's coronation and invoked the young King of Israel, Josiah, the boy king who radicalized Israelite worship – and thus the nation of Israel itself – by recovering its true nature and its proper piety. In doing so Cranmer asserted in vivid terms both the royal supremacy and his ambitions for Edward's exercise of those powers:

> Your Majesty is God's vicegerent and Christ's vicar within your own dominions, and to see, with your predecessor Josiah, God truly worshipped, and idolatry destroyed, the tyranny of the Bishops of Rome banished from your subjects, and images removed. These acts be signs of a second Josiah, who reformed the church of God in his days. You are to reward virtue, to revenge sin, to justify the innocent, to relieve the poor, to procure peace, to repress violence, and to execute justice throughout your realms. For precedents on those kings who performed not these things, the old law shows how the Lord revenged his quarrel; and on those kings who fulfilled these things, he poured forth his blessings in abundance. For example, it is written of Josiah in the book of the Kings thus;

'Like unto him there was no king before him, that turned to the Lord with all his heart, according to all the law of Moses, neither after arose there any like him.' This was to that prince a perpetual fame of dignity, to remain to the end of days . . . The Almighty God of his mercy let the light of his countenance shine upon your Majesty, grant you a prosperous and happy reign, defend you and save you: and let your subjects say, 'Amen'. God save the King![13]

Six years later, in 1553, the scale of his ambition for England's Josiah had been more fully revealed. We should not allow the passage of time to obscure the sheer reforming passion of the man, nor his central ambition that every English man and woman should know the Bible, know the God revealed in Christ it pointed to and know themselves justified by faith in him. England found itself in the position, never remotely dreamed of by even the most ardent reformer six years earlier, of being in the vanguard of continued Evangelical advance in Europe. There was cross-pollination between the great seats of European Protestant learning and the English universities; a set of official homilies advanced clear, Reformed, Christianity from pulpits across the land; altars had been replaced with simple communion tables for the observance of rites, which Zwingli's Zurich would have approved of; Bible and liturgy were in the vernacular, and accessible to ordinary lay Christians; every service, from communion to marriage and funerals, resonated with Evangelical doctrine, shorn of medieval 'excess'. The 42 articles of religion (a very Tudor way of pronouncing official religious policy), drawn up for promulgation and publication in early 1553, reflected the confidence and the proud identity of this renewed Church of England.

They were never released. Edward succumbed to tuberculosis in the summer of 1553. His ministers, at his instigation, had tried to avoid what they regarded as the calamity of Mary Tudor's accession, but popular opinion, always so strongly on the side of legitimacy and due order, overruled their eccentric scheme to place Jane Grey, the King's cousin, on the throne instead. Mary marched into London to cheering crowds and to dismayed privy councillors. Although always a wavering participant in the plan, Cranmer was only too aware that he was a marked man, not least as the Archbishop who had finally pronounced the King's marriage to Katherine of Aragon annulled. Her daughter had no compunction in sending him to the Tower and thence to Oxford, where he underwent his final, drawn-out and fearful drama.

*

So much for ambition. Let us conclude by speaking of faithfulness. Thomas Cranmer's own faithfulness was of a particular sort, but quite remarkable on its own terms, for all the proper criticisms he has received. Above all, one of the reasons he is so fascinating for historians, interested in the ways people grow and arrive at the full expression of their humanity, is that Cranmer was faithful in following the truth wherever it led him. He was committed to living in such a way that he allowed himself, his views, his beliefs and his actions to be changed in the light of what was revealed to him. This is not to say that we must believe exactly what he did, nor that Cranmer's understanding of what constituted truth was the only possible way of seeing the world. Rather, his life might be seen as a sort of icon of faithfulness, of being prepared to alter course or adjust our views when confronted with compelling evidence or reasons to do so. Like the poet Rilke, confronted with the beauty of an ancient sculpture, Cranmer advises us, when confronted with whatever it is that forces us to reassess what we've always believed, 'You must change your life.'

Some have seen the evolution of Cranmer's thought as evidence of vacillation or weakness. It is certainly true that, earlier in his career, he participated in or assented to the prosecution – never the persecution, in fairness – of those whose views he would later come to share, for instance on the theology of Holy

Communion. We cannot know how he subsequently reflected on these actions, nor of the ways he reconciled himself to them, if he ever did. But we can know something, thanks to the painstaking work of scholars, of the slow, definite and purposeful evolution of Cranmer's thought over time, and of the means by which, through rigorous study and constant prayer, he came to his mature theology. He was even prepared to confess to having been wrong and to having changed his mind. There is no one living who cannot relate to this experience in some area of their life, even and especially those in high office, charged with decision-making about complex and crucial areas of policy and exposed daily to more evidence and wider intelligence. And yet we are rarely able to praise the process in others. Cranmer's shifts of belief pose problems; but perhaps we should cherish them too, as evidence of someone prepared to be wrong, to grow, to have the courage to alter course – prepared to be human and to do so publicly.

We have already detailed Cranmer's marriages, the second of which was an area in which he could not be public but in which he was absolutely unwilling to compromise, still less cast off Margarete upon his unexpected promotion. It is hard not to be moved by Cranmer's faithfulness in this impossible situation: to his wife, and to the family he loved whose presence under King Henry was often a source of danger to them all and whom he therefore had to keep hidden while living himself as a rather 'closeted' Archbishop. Again, some see cowardice in this. Coward that I am, I'm minded to see something rather more beautiful: fidelity and costly love in very testing times. As others have pointed out, when Cranmer composed these exquisite words they were not merely words. They carry the stamp of experience. Perhaps that is why they have lasted so well:

> Dearly beloved friends, we are gathered together here in the sight of God, and in the face of this congregation, to join together this man and this woman in holy matrimony, which is an honourable estate instituted of God in Paradise, in the

time of man's innocency: signifying unto us the mystical union, that is betwixt Christ and his Church: which holy estate Christ adorned and beautified with his presence and first miracle that he wrought in Cana of Galilee, and is commended of Saint Paul to be honourable among all men, and is therefore not to be enterprized, nor taken in hand unadvisedly, lightly, or wantonly, to satisfy men's carnal lusts, and appetites, like brute beasts that have no understanding: but reverently, discreetly, advisedly, soberly, and in the fear of God: duly considering the causes for which Matrimony was ordained. One was the procreation of children, to be brought up in the fear and nurture of the lord, and praise of God. Secondly, it was ordained for a remedy against sin, and to avoid fornication, that such persons as have not the gift of continency, might marry, and keep themselves undefiled members of Christ's body. Thirdly, for the mutual society, help and comfort, that the one ought to have of the other, both in prosperity and adversity, into which holy estate these two persons present, come now to be joined.[14]

There are more timeless values too, to which Cranmer seems to have been faithful in an age of brutal politics, cut-throat jostling for position and unforgiving, implacable hostility towards those with whom you disagreed. These virtues aren't and weren't a question of being Catholic or Protestant but simply of being Christian, of being humane.

Virtues like mercy: we could think of the new Archbishop trying, actually rather hard, to find a way for Sir Thomas More to be offered a compromise and avoid the traitor's death to which he was heading. Initially his hope was that More's willingness to accede to the new marriage and succession Act as legal, coupled with his stated and genuine desire to retreat into a quiet and secluded retirement in Chelsea, could be enough to spare him from the oath acknowledging the King's supremacy in religious matters: something he had consistently refused to do, while maintaining his silence. Cranmer must have known, with an uncompromising narcissist like King Henry, that it was in vain, just as it was again later when he opposed More's execution. But he tried.

Thomas Cranmer gives us ample evidence, too, of his commitment to natural justice, insofar as it was within his power to influence things. His advocacy for the doomed Anne Boleyn has been a source of immense criticism of his alleged pusillanimity and spinelessness, but such readings of it fail to take account of the context and the delicacy of the situation. Boleyn, like More, was as good as dead when Cranmer, late to the intrigue, took up his pen to address the King. The forces ranged against Anne were too great; the King, persuaded of her serial adultery because he chose to be, was implacable; the Queen's outspokenness, forcefulness and confident demeanour had won her too many enemies. To those longing for further religious reform, however, she remained a vital force and a key ally. Nor was Cranmer the only one who saw the monstrous injustice of her treatment, though he was the only one to try to effect a change. Writing in the ingratiating, subservient tone that alone might work, his efforts at gentle persuasion are far more assertive than at first appears, and certainly the only tactic that stood even the smallest chance of success:

I cannot deny but your Grace hath great causes many ways of lamentable heaviness: and also that, in the wrongful estimation of the world, your Grace's honour of every part is highly touched (whether the things that commonly be spoken of be true or not), that I remember not that ever Almighty God sent unto your Grace any like occasion to try your Grace's constancy throughout, whether your Highness can be content to take of God's hand, as well things displeasant as pleasant . . . And if it be true, that is openly reported of the Queen's Grace, if men had a right estimation of things, they should not esteem any part of your Grace's honour to be touched thereby, but her honour only to be clearly disparaged. And I am in such a perplexity, that my mind is clean amazed: for I never had better opinion in woman than I had in her; which maketh me to think that she should not be culpable. And again, I think your highness would not have gone so far, except she had surely been culpable. Now I think that your Grace best knoweth, that, next unto your Grace, I was most bound unto her of all creatures living. Wherefore, I most humbly beseech your Grace, to suffer me in that, which both God's law, nature, and also her kindness bindeth me unto; that is, that I may with your Grace's favour, wish and pray for her, that she may declare herself inculpable and innocent.[15]

Compassion, too, in an age so often devoid of it, was a virtue close to Cranmer's heart. Late in the King's reign it fell to him to undertake the most 'displeasant' task of all, and inform the King of the very real and highly scandalous adulteries of the young Queen Katherine Howard. She had been immensely foolish and utterly reckless, beguiled by her own sudden rise to favour and the influence she now commanded. Still a teenager, she lacked any resources, natural wisdom or innate maturity, and her fall was spectacular and horrifying for those at court. Although Katherine's guilt was absolutely plain and her punishment universally felt to be deserved, the Archbishop himself continued to see her and pray with her, taking upon himself, amid the duties of state and Church, the role of pastor to someone *in extremis*. Fearing that her grief and terror would lead her to take her own life and therefore refusing to leave her alone, he described how he remained with her in the Tower:

It may please your Majesty to understand, that at my repair unto the Queen's Grace, I found herein such lamentation and heaviness, as I never saw no creature; so that it would have pitied any man's heart in the world to have looked upon her; and in that vehement rage she continued, as they informed me which be about her, from my departure from her unto my return again; and then I found her, as I do suppose, far entered toward a frenzy, which I feared before my departure from her at my first being with her; and surely, if your Grace's comfort had not come in time, she could have continued no long time in that condition without a frenzy, which, nevertheless, I do yet much suspect to follow hereafter . . . when I do see her in any such extreme brayds,[16] I do travail with her to know the cause, and then, as much as I can, I do labour to take away, or at the least to mitigate the cause; and so I did at that time . . . And for any thing that I could say unto her, she continued in a great pang a long while, but after that she began something to remit her rage and come to herself, she was meetly well until night, and I had very good communication with her, and, as I thought, had brought her unto a great quietness.[17]

This was a compassion and a humanity, seen again in Cranmer's theology. Even as his religious colleagues and contemporaries all across Europe, most infamously but by no means only Luther, wrote hateful treatises against the Jewish people and called for violence against them and their property and the eradication of their benighted faith, the Edwardian homilies pronounced a very different view, penned by the Archbishop himself:

God gave them [i.e. the Jews] the grace to be his children, as he doth us now. But now, by the coming of our saviour Christ we have received more abundantly the Spirit of God in our hearts, whereby we may conceive a greater faith, and a surer trust, than many of them had. But in effect they and we be all one: we have the save faith that they had in God, and they the same that we have.[18]

Undergirded by Cranmerian theology, the centuries of Christian anti-Jewish persecution and violence that followed and culminated in the twentieth-century murder of six million Jews would have been impossible.

Thomas Cranmer certainly, like all sixteenth-century people, held some views very strange to modern ears. Like all people of every age, he sometimes displayed the frailties and flaws common to all of us but more ruthlessly exposed in high office: vacillation, inconsistency (if indeed that is always a flaw), weakness. But there is a more striking fidelity that runs throughout his life and his achievements: a faithful capacity simply to take the next step, in the light of the best wisdom available to him, and trusting in God's provision, whether success or failure was the result. Indeed, this may be what holiness looks like.

Cranmer's faithfulness and his commitment to these virtues faced their severest test in his final months, when his ambitions, not primarily for himself but for the religion of the realm, were in tatters. He did, eventually and famously, briefly recant his Protestant views while under the most severe duress and pressure and amid crushing loneliness. He had been forced to witness the execution of his friends Nicholas Ridley and Hugh Latimer, burned in front of Oxford's crowds while he watched from the roof of the Bocardo jail. He had been publicly humiliated, deprived of his office and even his priesthood in a degrading ceremony in Oxford Cathedral. The authorities had relentlessly pursued him and deprived him of the company of the few friends he had left in order to break him down through psychological torture. As he signed the recantation, the Marian authors took up pens to celebrate his return to the fold, even as the Queen took up hers to sign his death warrant anyway. She was determined to avenge the degradation and humiliation of her mother, Katherine of Aragon, Henry's first wife; and those around Mary, as is the way of things in our human spirals of violence, saw Cranmer's death as imperative to atone for the murders of More and Fisher.

In the end, in fact, Cranmer's defiant death more than undid the understandable indecision of his final days, denied the Marian authorities their propaganda victory and gave posterity – in the shape of the waiting John Foxe – one of the greatest martyr dramas of all time. He didn't live, like Simeon in the Gospel of Luke, to see the absolute realization of his vision, but long enough to prove the test of the holiness just described. Recanting his recantations in St Mary's Church in Oxford, undermining the staged purpose of this event, and whisked away through rainy Oxford to the stake, even there, bitterly bewailing his weakness and inconstancy, Cranmer repeatedly plunged his right hand into the fire. It had caused the trouble; it should pay the price. If it is possible to strip away the narrow religious acrimony at the surface of this moment, it becomes an extraordinary illustration of how even human frailty, when shot through with courage and faith, becomes something touching to behold. In this, at least, Cranmer's death did indeed mirror More's.

Let us end with his last surviving written words, a letter to a friend in Europe, words that radiate the faith and the faithfulness of the man and may speak to us too, today, as we in the early twenty-first century, like Cranmer in 1555, wonder how we are supposed to live in the midst of a world made strange by human folly:

> [There is] one thing, which I have learned by experience, namely, that God never shines forth more brightly, and pours out the beams of his mercy and consolation . . . more clearly or impressively upon the minds of his people, than when they are under the most extreme pain and distress . . . that he may then more especially show himself to be the God of his people, when he seems to have altogether forsaken them; then raising them up when they think he is bringing them down, and laying them low; then glorifying them, when he is thought to be confounding them; then quickening them, when he is thought to be destroying them. So that we may say with Paul, 'When I am weak, then I am strong; and if I must needs glory, I will glory in my infirmities . . .' I pray God to grant that I may endure to the end.[19]

In our just ambitions for the future of our world, in our desire steadfastly to live in and for the causes in which we believe while being open to growth and new insight, in our hopes to be found faithful in our generation as Thomas Cranmer was in his, may God bless us. And may God bless him.

3

A Tudor Woman's Passion: Anne Askew

Dare to
declare
who you
are. It
isn't
far from
the shores
of silence
to the
boundaries
of speech.
The road
is not
long but
the way
is deep.
And you
must not
only
walk there,
you must
be prepared
to leap.[20]

During my time as an undergraduate studying theology, I had
a tutorial on the early Church with the Cambridge University
Divinity Faculty specialist on the subject, for which I had to

write an essay on 'The roles available to women in the early Church'. It was a fairly brief essay, but I did my best. At the end my supervisor upbraided me for failing to mention martyrdom as a role available to women in the early Church. I confess I found this strange. I didn't think that too many of the women of the early Church would have been going to the equivalent of their careers guidance people, wanting to investigate martyrdom as a role open to them.

But of course, when martyrdom is one of the very limited ways you can actually offer a witness to your faith in difficult circumstances, it assumes a greater significance. And I came to realize that the same was true in the Reformation era too, in which rival historians on both the main sides of that cataclysmic debate sought to claim true martyrdom for their own people. In England, in particular, the question of gender was also a crucial element of this, particularly after the causes of first Catholicism and then Protestantism became so dependent on and indissolubly bound up with England's first two queens regnant, Mary Tudor and her half-sister Elizabeth. This chapter, however, offers us a peek at the ways this question was being worked out, several years before Mary Tudor's reign.

Anne Askew is a pivotal figure in the construction of martyrdom in the English Protestant Reformation. Her story, and the use made of it by the male editors of her testimony, have been much discussed and commented on in recent years, not least by those who see her as critical in the examination of early modern gender identity and role. Indeed, the focus on Anne and her witness has become increasingly a literary one, such that – sometimes anyway – the religious power of her story in its context has been obscured. This chapter therefore seeks to offer a slight corrective to that, not to say anything devastatingly new but perhaps to put some observations together in a rather new way in relation to a woman whose character, motivation and historical reality have been often disputed and discussed.

Anne Askew was born in Lincolnshire in 1521, the daughter

of a well-to-do family with good connections. Married off by her father to one Thomas Kyme, she had two children by him and must have appeared to have been adopting a conventional approach to her life, amid the very limited choices available to her as an early sixteenth-century woman. But Anne was undergoing a religious conversion, made possible, ironically, by the changes in official religious policy and practice in England at the time. At the height of their powers, Thomas Cromwell, King Henry VIII's 'vicegerent' or chief minister in spiritual matters, and Thomas Cranmer, the Archbishop of Canterbury, had finally secured approval in the late 1530s for a Bible in English, published under the King's authority and available in every parish church: the so-called 'Great' Bible, part of whose preface was reproduced in the previous chapter. Literate people across the land could go to church and read the text of Scripture for themselves. For Anne, the experience was transformative, and her exposure to the text of the English Bible led her to begin to reject elements of the country's still conservative religion, and especially the English Church's beliefs about the Mass, which she found contrary to biblical witness.

However, those like Anne, won over to the cause of reform by the reading of these public Scriptures, as Cromwell and Cranmer intended them to be, soon found themselves isolated by Cromwell's fall from grace in 1540, Cranmer's marginalization at court and the regime's subsequent retreat to a much more religiously conservative position. The Act for the Advancement of True Religion in 1543 forbade women, among others, from reading the Bible, either privately or publicly. The vicissitudes of Henrician policy, as first one and then another faction at court gained the upper hand, had profound consequences for people like Anne Askew, who found that their newly discovered religious confidence and convictions could not so easily be repressed again. What made Anne so remarkable is that she refused quietly to comply. She staged an act of civil disobedience against the law.

In Lincoln Minster, probably soon after the Act was passed,

Anne took up residence for six days, and deliberately, publicly and openly read the Bible. The priests of the chapter were clearly a little unclear how to deal with this challenge to their and the law's authority, and were apparently quite reluctant to engage her directly during her 'read-in' at the cathedral, though a couple of brave souls did and seemed to realize very quickly that they were no match for Anne's intellect and insight. Ultimately the cathedral authorities decided to deal with the problem as all brave and reasonable men do – by telling Anne's husband to do something about her. When he tried, she refused to capitulate. Whether she left home or was thrown out is a matter of dispute for reasons we'll return to; suffice it to say that she left, citing 2 Corinthians 6.14 on not being unequally yoked, and made her way to London, where influential friends with reforming commitments supported her.

In London, as part of a circle of Evangelical gentlewomen with connections all the way to Queen Katherine Parr, Anne soon made a name for herself as a Reformer and thus soon came to the attention of more senior courtiers, who may have hoped, in prosecuting her, to trap and bring down the Queen herself. It's here that Anne enters the historical record, because of the work of John Bale. Bale, a former Carmelite and convert to Protestantism himself, had gone into exile after the fall of Cromwell, one of an often-forgotten group whose reforming tendencies had left them very exposed to the conservative backlash in the early 1540s. In 1546 and 1547, still in exile at the end of Henry's reign, he published two accounts of Anne's treatment at the hands of England's civic and ecclesiastical authorities that consisted of what he claimed were her own words, interspersed with his elucidation of or commentary on them. Anne's testimony, Bale said, was smuggled out of London to him via Dutch merchants, enabling him to put her experiences in the public domain – and create a new genre of Protestant martyrology.

Anne's account is of two 'examinations' before various diocesan and legal figures in London, in 1545 and 1546, published by Bale as the *First Examination* and *Latter Examination* in 1546 and 1547 respectively. Just six months before Henry VIII's death she was interrogated on at least three occasions about her beliefs, lifestyle and loyalty. The questioning became ever more hostile until finally she was ruthlessly – and quite unlawfully – tortured on the rack by the Lord Chancellor, Thomas Wriothesley, and Sir Richard Rich, the time-serving counsellor to the King whose almost certainly false testimony had, ironically, secured the condemnation of Sir Thomas More eleven years earlier. Eventually Anne was burned at the stake as a heretic at Smithfield on 16 July 1546.

Much of the scholarly interest in Anne's life and testimony naturally and rightly has focused on her treatment at the hands of her editors. Bale, her first champion, published the *Examinations* soon after her death as part of his campaign against the Catholic resurgence in England at the end of Henry's reign. The way he chops up Anne's words, frequently interjecting his own extensive commentary on them, has come in for particular criticism in recent work. Indeed, it is the first thing one notices on reading the books, giving the clear sense of a sometimes rather tiresome process in which a woman cannot be trusted to make adequate sense on her own and needs the help of her male publisher and editor to make her purpose clear. So one commentator has censured Bale for subsuming Anne's voice into his programme, and another has called Anne's testimony 'unsatisfying', made 'too interior' in Bale's hands, lacking the force of a more strident male witness as her own meanings are 'reassigned' at his hands.[21] Yet a third describes Bale's 'agenda' in editing Anne's accounts of events, 'the extent of which [editing] it is impossible to establish with any certainty'.[22] Thomas Freeman and Sarah Wall do not dissent from this assessment, and seek to make a similar point in relation to Anne's later treatment at the hands of John Foxe. In his massive *Acts and Monuments* of 1563, Foxe included Anne's story without commentary; as they contend, however, Foxe, no less than Bale, is exercising editorial agency in what he chooses to highlight and what is played down, as we shall see.[23] Even Diane Watt, who I think accurately sees Bale's purpose where some do not, nevertheless criticizes both Bale and Foxe for an account of Anne that 'glossed over her powerful and independent personality'.[24] All in all, many scholars see Anne Askew as the victim of the men who later sought to make her witness public and give her a voice, albeit through their own pens.

The basic insight here should not be disputed, of course: it is certainly true that the search to recover the 'real' Anne Askew from underneath the editing of her male champions sometimes feels almost as fraught as that for the 'historical' Jesus. And as many commentators have pointed out, the way the editors go about their work and make their emphases, however closely they stick to Anne's own sense of things, is very instructive and ought not to be ignored. But we can go further. If we assume that Bale is indeed basing his work on the actual words of Anne Askew or something very close to them (which few scholars would dispute), then we might postulate that he at least is attempting a very bold approach and a quite daring strategy in presenting her to the reading public. And it's an approach that actually mirrors Anne's own in ways subsequent editors and publicists of her writings were loath to follow. Although some have identified it almost in passing, Bale's interpretation of the life and death of Anne Askew picks up and amplifies something she herself had daringly suggested, namely that her witness, suffering and death were nothing less than Christlike. It was a claim and an interpretation from which later editors, beginning with Foxe, seem to have distanced themselves, and it's therefore worthy of our attention and of an effort to understand what Anne and her first editor thought they were doing.

This might seem bold; it might therefore be helpful to place Bale's project in its historical literary context. We assume, because of the great success of Foxe's later *Acts and Monuments* (usually known as the 'Book of Martyrs'), that Protestants have always had their own accounts of those who died for their version of Christianity, which they take to be the true one. But in 1546 that wasn't so. John Bale is often described as a rather secondary and unimportant figure in English Protestantism,[25] and it's certainly true that his writing can be laborious, tiresome and can grind its axes so loudly as to be faintly ludicrous. But when he published his editions of Anne Askew's *Examinations* he was doing a quite new thing: he was inventing an English Protestant martyrology, building on the foundation of his first tentative publication in 1544 concerning the fourteenth-century Lollard John Oldcastle. Bale was in a sense creating a new genre, and it also had to be able to go head-to-head with Catholic hagiographies: the medieval cult of the saints, the colourful stories of the *Golden Legend*, the myriad images, shrines and pilgrimage sites that proliferated and offered such vivid, memorable and immediate examples of what holiness looked like. As Margaret Aston says, Bale's project 'meant taking over enemy territory, and using enemy ammunition.'[26]

Bale attempted this exercise by clearly spelling out the parameters within which he sought to construct this new Protestant understanding of martyrdom and sainthood. To begin with he adopted a rather esoteric, seven-stage reading of apocalyptic Scriptures that was indebted to the controversial twelfth-century theologian Joachim of Fiore, and strove to demonstrate a 'postmillennial' decline in the purity of the Church from the early medieval period onwards. In other words, the corruption of the Roman Catholic Church was a sign of Christ's incipient reign on earth. It was an approach later shared by John Foxe, to claim that the few reformers in every generation were the witnesses to true, ancient Christianity, in the face of Roman Catholic corruption and decay. This meant also that Bale and Foxe looked to early Church martyrs as being the best kinds of examples of true martyrdom on which to draw for illustrative purposes. Thus he offers a rather extended comparison of Anne Askew with Blandina, a second-century martyr under Marcus Aurelius, whose story is told in Eusebius' *Ecclesiastical History*. Although he could have chosen others, whose circumstances more closely mirrored Anne's, Bale almost certainly avoided them because, as in the case of Catherine of Alexandria, they had become too closely associated with the medieval cult of saints and were too much connected with papal approval and patronage.[27]

In the *Examinations*, Bale further elucidates his criteria for discerning true martyrdom: the ones whose deaths have the ring of authenticity will be like sheep among wolves; they will have been imprisoned before being 'brought forth into councils and synagogues' for trial; they will have spoken by God's Spirit and been 'reviled, mocked, stocked, racked, executed, condemned and murdered' by their oppressors. And these oppressors will have been spiritual leaders: Bale dismisses the bulk of English martyrs by claiming that, like Thomas à Becket, they were merely 'monastery builders and chantry founders' who were disloyal to their rulers and deserved punishment, unlike the true 'preachers of the gospel', who are invariably killed by senior clergy and Church authorities.[28] Bale finally asserts the key rule of Protestant saints, that they win their canonization by giving their lives for true religion and not for any spurious miracles that they may have performed or their relics may be said to induce.[29]

Clearly, in all this Bale was attempting to tread a fine line, claiming some prior, Roman Catholic categories and images of sainthood while seeking also to demonstrate that those who truly die for the gospel will be easily distinguishable from the mass of the medieval saints: men and women associated in his mind with ceremony and the paraphernalia of their own cult, claims of the miraculous, treachery towards monarchs and rulers, and the upholding of the papacy. Some writers see more elements of the medieval past retained in Bale's approach than do others: Bale had a former life as a Catholic hagiographer, which surely merged into his new vocation as a Protestant martyrologist. His version of Anne Askew's life thus may retain elements of one of his previous publications, a Life of St Anne, the mother of the Virgin Mary.[30] Others rightly emphasize how biblical saints and those from the early Church – Anna, Elizabeth, Mary Magdalene, Lydia, Stephen, Cecilia and Blandina – as well as biblical figures such as the Virtuous Woman of Proverbs chapter 8 and the Woman

Clothed in the Sun of Revelation chapter 12, are all used by Bale to make comparison with Anne.[31] Bale's own iconography in his edition of the *Examinations* certainly borrows from prior tradition, portraying Anne holding the palm of the martyrs.

Bale, though, as we have already seen, goes even further, and in doing so picks up on cues and hints that seem to be in Anne's own testimony. In seeking to establish her at the fountainhead of a new English martyrology, he explicitly and consistently compares her experiences, her behaviour, her demeanour, her tactics, her strategy and her treatment to those of Christ himself. And although a few commentators have noticed elements of the comparison, I do not think they have noticed their consistency or their power, nor the ways they suggest a clear line of agreement, in fact, between Anne herself and John Bale's treatment of and commentary on her text. At the risk of tedium, let us examine the evidence.

The first clear hint of Anne Askew as a Christ figure comes in her own account of her first interrogation in March 1545. Asked by Christopher Dare, one of the council, about the nature of Christ's presence in the sacrament, she replies by asking him why Stephen was stoned to death. This produces a stalemate, but the reference to Christianity's first martyr and the account of his death in Acts 6 and 7, with all its parallels to Anne's own situation, should not blind us to the tactic, which is exactly that adopted by Jesus in Mark 11.28–33 and elsewhere. Asked a question designed to trap him, Jesus replies with another equally likely to trap his accusers. Not for nothing did Anne spend so much time reading her Scriptures in Lincoln Cathedral. She adopts the same strategy a little later when questioned by Bishop Edmund Bonner of London.[32]

More commonly still, Anne tells us that she chose to remain silent in the face of hostile questioning, both from clergy and from the civic authorities. In the *First Examination* she refuses to answer a priest sent to question her on the Mass, and then does likewise when sent to the Lord Mayor, who pursues the same line. 'Whereunto', she says, 'I made them no answer, but smiled.' On this occasion Bale drives the comparison home by reminding the reader that Christ also was sent from a religious to a secular figure for questioning, remaining silent before both. In the *Latter Examination*, Anne again resorts to silence when challenged about her separation from her husband, something quite unusual and potentially problematic for her at the time.[33]

Anne's rhetorical strategies also include other approaches to critique and interrogation very similar to those of Jesus in the Gospels. Rebuked by the Bishop of London's chancellor for uttering the Scriptures against the express commands of Paul, she proves that she knows the Scriptures better than him by reminding him that Paul's prohibition is of teaching during public worship, something she has never attempted. There are shades here of Jesus challenging his accusers to know their Scriptures better, as in Matthew 12, Luke 20 and elsewhere. Later on in the *Latter Examination*, Bishop Stephen Gardiner of Winchester himself, the leading conservative at court and a man of great influence, grows frustrated with Anne's language and accuses her of speaking in parables. Bale is swift to pounce:

> Most commonly Christ used to speak in dark similitudes and parables, when he perceived his audience rather given to the hearing of pharisaical constitutions [i.e. hypocritical regulations] and customs, rather than to his heavenly verity ... which rule this woman being his true disciple forgot not here...[34]

On multiple occasions, apparently taking his cue from Anne's own often more subtle but nonetheless striking example, Bale likens her to Christ by drawing a comparison with her opponents and the diversity of those who at various times opposed him. So when she is in solitary confinement during her first investigation, and an ostensibly friendly priest comes to her, Bale likens him to Satan making his first temptation of Christ in the wilderness, or to Judas with his friendly kiss, on which occasions Jesus' enemies tried to disarm him with kindness. Or when offered a priest to whom she might make confession, Bale draws comparisons with Matthew 22 or John 8, in which the Pharisees try to draw Jesus into a legal trap. In any case, Anne's dismissal of him 'because I perceive you come to tempt me' mirrors Jesus' own rejection of Satan in the wilderness, a comparison Bale also returns to later in characterizing the repeated efforts made by Edmund Bonner to trick her into an admission of her heterodoxy.[35]

More than any group, of course, it is to the Jewish religious authorities who sought the death of Jesus that Anne's own persecutors are compared. The senior clergy of the Church of England, and in particular Bishop Edmund Bonner of London and Bishop Stephen Gardiner of Winchester, are cast in the role of the chief priests and teachers of the Law. Bonner was himself imprisoned under Edward VI and restored to the See of London under Mary; Gardiner, having failed in his bid to overthrow Cranmer under Henry VIII, rejoiced in his subsequent chance to do so when he served as Mary's Lord Chancellor in the 1550s. Bonner is several times called 'this Caiaphas' by Bale, and on one occasion, when he is trying to reassure Anne that no harm will come to her for being honest, Bale also likens him to King Herod, the 'crafty fox' who dealt with both Jesus and John the Baptist at the ends of their lives. In the *Latter Examination*, Gardiner takes on the High Priest role, becoming, in Bale's memorable phrase, 'the great Caiaphas'. Anne herself had just a little earlier compared Gardiner to Judas to his face, after he pretended to treat her with kindness, talk to her 'familiarly' and take her into his confidence. She refuses his blandishments and his offer of a private conversation, all too aware of the dangers of the uncorroborated testimony that might ensue.[36]

Bale is clear that the way the priests of England's apostate Church deal with Anne and the way the Jewish leaders dealt with Jesus are clearly parallel and that thus her ordeals and suffering, even before her torture and death, absolutely mirror those of Jesus himself and stake her claim to a Christlike witness. Referring to her six-day sojourn in Lincoln and to the treatment she received then from the priests of the cathedral chapter, he writes (betraying his sixteenth-century anti-Jewishness, unpleasant but almost universally shared – though not by Thomas Cranmer, as we noted):

> Herein follow [their lordships] the examples of their natural predecessors the Jewish bishops, Pharisees and priests (John 7 and 9). She might full well say, that the priests were against her. For hypocrisy and idolatry were never yet with him, whose blessed quarrel she took. Mark the fourth chapter of John, and so forth almost to the end of his Gospel. Behold also how his Apostles and disciples were handled of the priests, after his glorious ascension (Acts 4) and all that book following, and you shall find it no new thing. The servant is no better than her master which suffered of that malignant generation like quarrels and handlings, John 15. See here how they wondered upon her by couples, for reading the Bible, as their forefathers wondered upon Christ for preaching and doing miracles.[37]

All of this, though, is but preparatory material for what we might call Anne's real imitation of Christ: her final passion and death. Both Anne and Jesus, Bale asserts, were tormented by 'prelates, priests and lawyers' to the point of death, because both of them: were accused of heresy; were thought to break religious law; were suspected of subverting the opinions of the people in religious matters; and threatened to destroy the Temple and with it the established patterns of religious observance, belief and behaviour. And he adds for good measure that the Gospels also demonstrate to us that women have always been much better equipped to follow Christ, understand his message and uphold his cause, when male religious leaders and clergy have so often proved themselves clueless and useless.[38]

Anne's own account of her racking in the Tower by Wriothesley and Rich is, like the Gospel accounts of the moment of crucifixion, pared down to absolute simplicity: 'they took pains to rack me their own hands, till I was nigh dead'. Stretched out on the rack, one might almost say like one stretched on a cross, Bale recalls her recollection that she did not cry during this terrible torture, and likens her to a lamb, a biblical image of striking power. Addressing her persecutors, he says, in words redolent of Isaiah 53, later interpreted in Acts 8 as being about Jesus:

> Like a lamb she lay still without noise of crying, and suffered your uttermost violence, till the sinews of her arms were broken, and the strings of her eyes perished in her head . . . Think not therefore but that Christ hath suffered in her . . .[39]

Bale is building to his climax, which comes in Anne's execution at Smithfield. Here we can be in no doubt about the parallel he is constructing. Anne prays for her persecutors, that God might forgive them. 'She showeth the nature of Christ's lively member' as she does so, Bale claims, and goes to her brutal death. As she is executed by fire, the clouds darken and there is a thunderstorm. Like the centurion at the cross, many in the crowd are converted by the spectacle of her death and the steadfast courage of her approach to it. He may indeed be overegging it slightly when he adds that Stephen was less favoured at his martyrdom, being given a vision he alone could see and the spectators could not, and in his assertion that even Jesus himself met a more benign secular ruler in Pilate, who refused to condemn him, than did Anne in Wriothesley, who tortured her himself. Be that as it may, Bale's elucidation of what is already present in Anne's own description and understanding of the nature of her experiences is striking. This is nothing less than a passion. Anne is no less a figure than Christ.

Let us draw some conclusions. Diane Watt, in a fascinating and rather groundbreaking study of women's prophecy, which worked across confessional and historical divisions, pointed out

20 years ago the striking character of this narrative (her acute and insightful observations have been rather played down or brushed aside more recently in scholarship on Anne Askew). Here we might wish to differ from her in two respects. First, she asserts a continuity between late medieval and early modern patterns of constructing sainthood. While it's true that historians have been too keen to impose artificial boundaries in this way, we should not lose sight of the radical newness of Bale's undertaking. He is employing Anne not only to give a model of female Protestant martyrdom but to be the fountainhead of a whole new genre of sainthood for Protestants of both genders and all types. It is a bold and ambitious endeavour, and he is at pains *not* to be seen to be merely building on the medieval pattern of devotion but to be recovering a more authentic set of criteria for discerning holiness. To do this he returns, like a good humanist, like a good Protestant, to sources: the Scriptures above all, and the earliest centuries of the Church's life. Anne Askew represents the best example he can find, whose testimony we have *in her own words*, of what he seeks. And the extent to which he presents her sufferings and her witness as Christlike underscores the importance in his mind of this project. Nothing more authentic can be found to indicate holiness than that. If Anne is to be just about the first contemporary example of true English martyrdom, she'd better be a good one. And her story, as she tells it herself and as Bale interprets it, is better than good: it's Christlike.

Second, and more briefly, we could also dissent from Watt's assertion that Bale 'glossed over [Anne's] powerful and independent personality'. She herself adopts different strategies at different times, at one point claiming the weakness of her gender in dispute with powerful prelates, at another giving them as good as she got. We can't really fault him for doing the same. What seems remarkable is the extent to which he praises her independence and authority, given the patriarchy amid which she lived and he wrote. Beneath the tediousness of his tone and his polemics, Bale is actually subverting all kinds of assumptions about the place and role of women in his society and in the Church. He seems to be taking his cue in that from Anne herself.

We might see something of Bale's boldness, too, in comparing his treatment of her with that of John Foxe, whose *Acts and Monuments*, far more widely read by subsequent generations in part because the Elizabethan authorities placed one in every church alongside the Bible, really brought Anne Askew to a reading public. Many find Foxe's lack of commentary on Anne's own words a breath of fresh, liberating air after the constrained stuffiness of Bale's rantings and assertions. But as Freeman and Wall remind us, Foxe is editing her words just as much. And Foxe plays down many of those elements that made Anne so uncomfortable a figure for respectable sixteenth-century society. Freeman and Wall suggest that her separation from her husband was a key factor in this, as it was something Catholic polemicists made much of in their later attacks on her character. It was also exactly the kind of behaviour that Foxe, a pillar of Protestant ethical rectitude, is known himself to have found immoral and irreligious in women. Further, by the 1570 edition of the book, they claim, Foxe had other goals in sight, and rearranged the Anne Askew material to make quite different points about Elizabethan religious policy, and not the character of martyrdom itself. Indeed, although Bale has been described by his biographer as a 'mythmaker', it seems that it was John Foxe who did the real mythmaking with Anne Askew, turning, in Freeman and Wall's phrase, this 'potentially subversive figure' into 'an effective icon for the causes *he* cherished'.[40] Anne's subversiveness was on full display in Bale's account, and indeed was not the most controversial aspect of the claims he made for her.

The real and radical nature of Bale's advocacy for Anne Askew in a patriarchal age, and of the way he gave a bold public voice to a woman of remarkable confidence and self-belief, is thrown into even starker relief when we travel further forward in time and encounter another of her male editors. The second volume of John Wesley's *Christian Library*, which came out in 1749, was a highly edited and condensed version of Foxe's *Acts and Monuments*. Wesley wanted to follow up on the early Church martyrdoms from the first volume with something similar, English and closer in history. As he said in the preface, Foxe's martyrs would give his readers an opportunity to 'see this [i.e. early] Christianity reduced to *practice*'. He went on: 'may we learn from these worthies, to be not almost only, but altogether Christians!' Alas, Wesley's Anne has nothing subversive about her whatsoever. The first-person account, in her own words, which survived right through to Foxe's fourth, 1583 edition, has gone, replaced with a dull third-person narrative interspersed with a couple of her letters and confessions. And Wesley consistently refers to her as 'Mrs Askew', either unable or unwilling to acknowledge that Askew is her maiden name, which she never relinquished, and that her husband, Mr Kyme, was her first persecutor.[41] The commentary of John Bale, for all its axe-grinding, starts to seem infinitely preferable. For all Wesley's celebrated – and admittedly contested – encouragement of the ministry of women, he wasn't really ready for the radical and subversive example of Anne Askew, apparently.

*

In our own time, Professor Nicola Slee has written movingly of the 'search' for female representations of and identification with Christ in Christian history.[42] At Easter 2017 she was in New York to give a lecture for the installation of Edwina Sandys's controversial statue, entitled *Christa*, in the cathedral of St John the Divine. Sandys's *Christa* depicts a naked female figure stretched out in crucifixion, and has very few echoes in Christian history. When found, these images are hauntingly memorable and movingly impactful. At the seventeenth-century Loreta shrine in Prague one is surprised to come upon the life-size statue of St Wilgefortis, one of those medieval saints so beloved of Catholic pilgrims. Pursued by wealthy suitors, who would bring riches and status to her family, she wanted only a celibate life of prayer. Wilgefortis begged for divine aid. Thinking rather 'on his feet', God caused her to grow a miraculous beard, only for her very worldly father to crucify her in his fury and frustration. The creators of the Loreta have honoured her with the statue in a side chapel and, more recently, in a full-length portrait on a staircase. This bearded, crucified woman is an odd vision, for sure, and one that John Bale would have detested, so full of the miraculous and monastic overtones that he saw as signs of Antichrist.

For all that, Bale's Anne Askew does something quite similar in a very different way and to a rather different and even more powerful purpose. Here we have an English Protestant Christa, who is intended to stand as the epitome of faithful Christian witness for all believers, male and female. She exemplifies what feminist scholars like Nicola have called 'Christic' witness: the possibility of a faithfulness to Jesus and to Christianity that defies gendered boundaries and obstacles. Her account of her passion, and the work of her first editor and champion at least, offer a surprising glimpse into the roles and possibilities that might have been open to women in the English Reformation, even if they were not the daughter of Henry VIII. If, as Bale claims, 'she showed the nature of Christ's lively member', if indeed she showed what it might truly look like to imitate Christ, then he was offering a radical new understanding of the possibilities and power of women's witness to Christian faith. Anne Askew's intelligence, courage, wit and dignity point away from herself, not only to undreamed-of possibilities for the gifts of all Christians to be welcomed, shared and exercised, but above all to Christ himself, in whom, as Paul wrote, all barriers, divisions and exclusions have met their end.

4

Manifold Passions: Katherine Parr

Becoming the sixth wife of King Henry VIII was hardly the most attractive of assignments. In 1543, when Katherine Parr took up that role, she was 30, and it had been a long time since the King had made a happy or harmonious marriage: her immediate predecessor, the young, vain but ill-equipped Katherine Howard, had been executed 15 months earlier for a string of adulterous liaisons. Before her, Anne of Cleves had briefly assumed the role of Henry's consort in 1540, before his dissatisfaction with her physical appearance ended the marriage and provoked the downfall and execution of Thomas Cromwell, the titan of Henry's inner circle and reformer of English Christianity, who had arranged it. By the time Katherine married the King, it had been seven years since the death of Jane Seymour, the only woman whose affections, character and childbearing capacity had ever seemed to satisfy him. She must have known therefore that she was entering dangerous territory, and a public role heavy with responsibility and fraught with difficulty and the constant threat of humiliation and even death. Remarkably, however, for the three and a half years she was Queen, she not only survived but did more than any other individual in the King's final years to promote healing and reconciliation in the royal family and concord and harmony in the realm. She published in her own name, perhaps the first Englishwoman to do so, and, insofar as she could, promoted reform in religious affairs in ways that, while she was Queen at least, brought opposing factions together rather than driving them farther apart. For three months in 1554, while Henry was in France, she ruled the kingdom in his name, chosen above all the (male) courtiers who would have assumed that their claims were prior. She even made a thoroughly good job of it, winning her husband's approbation and the affections of her people.

It thus becomes clear quite quickly that whatever attracted Henry to his last wife (and certainly her great physical beauty was something to do with it), her wisdom, wit and mature good sense were not lost on him. These were virtues she had honed in the fires of some very testing times indeed. Henry was her third husband, despite her relative youth, and she was no stranger to situations of great danger, nor to the threat of death at the hands of powerful enemies. She was well used to having to draw on her own resources while facing challenges alone, and had had to protect herself and her family several times without the presence of the men in her life upon whom, in her time and place, she was expected to rely. Above all, Katherine was a Renaissance woman: intellectually gifted, thoughtful and insightful, quick-witted, a speaker of several languages and an avid reader and able scholar. When she married the King it was her youngest stepdaughter, the Princess Elizabeth, who seems to have benefited most from the gifts and graces of this extraordinary woman, who was the closest thing to a mother she was ever to enjoy. Indeed, Elizabeth's own preferences in and approaches to religion, so controversial to those around her at times, look and feel very much like those of her stepmother, 15 years before Elizabeth acceded to the throne in 1558. In this, and in the witness of her courageous and persistent character, Katherine's legacy is thus rather more significant than has been realized.

Katherine's connections to royalty were both genetic and circumstantial. She was a multiple cousin of the King but her mother, Maud, had also been a lady-in-waiting to Henry's first wife, Katherine of Aragon. This was a relationship she was later to exploit. Born in 1512 to family with roots in Cumbria, she was raised at Rye House in Hertfordshire. Her father Thomas died when she was only a small child, and her mother took upon herself the care and education of Katherine and her two siblings, seeking in time, as a good mother of the time did, to arrange favourable marriages for her children. Katherine's excellent and rigorous education, then, must have seemed somewhat superfluous to her when, in 1529, she was married off to the young Edward Borough, from a Lincolnshire family, and took up residence, aged just 16, in Gainsborough Old Hall. Borough was in his early twenties and known to be of extremely delicate health. His family had a long history of serious mental health problems, which had recently included a grandfather whose insanity had required that he be locked up in the attic. Edward's father was overbearing, draconian and ill-tempered, and thought Katherine's enthusiasm for learning and knowledge a frivolous and inappropriate pursuit for a woman whose only job was to give him grandchildren. Her husband was terrified of his father. Alone, far from anything familiar, still an adolescent and bereft of friends and comfort, she must have assumed that this, or something rather like it, would be her life.

Katherine and Edward were eventually able to move into their own home, probably through her ingenuity and determination, but in 1531 her mother died unexpectedly, leaving Katherine even more isolated. In Spring 1533 her always-frail husband also died. Only 20 years old, she was already an orphan and a widow. Her future relied on her own resources of grit and determination – and on her resilient faith. Her later words, published in 1545 as her *Prayers or Meditations*, reflect the grief and anxiety of these times and the way the uncertainty and precariousness of her situation threw her back on the one constant in her life: her God.

> I am poor, and have been in trouble and pain ever from my youth, and my soul hath been in great heaviness through manifold passions that come of the world and of the flesh; wherefore, Lord, I desire that I may have of thee the joy of inward peace.[43]

Faced with this turn of events and doubtless somewhat relieved to be free of her domineering father-in-law at least, Katherine's next marital choice might seem to be one entirely characterized by a shrewd and calculating assessment of where security lay. In fact her marriage to John Neville, Lord Latimer, was not devoid of real and lasting affection, despite the fact that he was, at 40, twice her age, had been married twice before and already had two small children. Still, she moved to his family home, Snape Castle in Yorkshire, probably in mid-1534, and did her best to assume her responsibilities there, especially in relation to John and Margaret, Latimer's children. Katherine's abilities as a step-parent, an especially tricky and difficult role, were second to none, and the wisdom with which she built relationships with her first stepchildren was later seen also in her dealings with the three royal offspring whose mother she became. The Neville son, John, was dissolute, violent and unteachable, but, with her stepdaughter Margaret, Katherine developed an affection and intimacy that was to grow with the years.

Nothing in her previous experience, however, could have prepared the young Lady Latimer for what was to come next. The great upheavals that King Henry's divorce from Katherine of Aragon were causing in England, and especially his decision in the early 1530s to sever the English Church's tie with the papacy, were bitterly resisted by many more traditionalist Catholics. There was a particular animus against the King's religious policy in the North: in a pattern not without its modern parallels, London's metropolitan 'elite' was felt to be out of step with the desires and opinions of those who lived elsewhere. The pre-eminence of figures like Thomas Cromwell and Queen Anne Boleyn at court, with their known reforming and even Protestant tendencies and affections, led many to fear that the changes made in religious affairs tended towards more far-reaching ones that would lead England even further away from its Roman Catholic character. Even Queen Anne's execution did not allay such suspicions. In 1536, in Louth in Lincolnshire, a group of men decided to offer more than token resistance to religious innovation. A comparable body of rebels arose in Yorkshire. In both places the protestors knew they needed the support and resources of the rich and powerful, and they were not above coercion in order to gain them. One of those in their sights, whose influence they coveted, was John Neville, Lord Latimer.

The Pilgrimage of Grace, as it became known, represented the greatest threat to the reign of Henry VIII and was a moment of real fear and vulnerability for the regime. Country gentry allied themselves with ordinary working men to demand a return to traditional religion and to seek assurances about the future direction of policy, particularly in church affairs. As the movement gathered pace and energy, and as its numbers swelled, Henry's council grew increasingly uneasy and insecure. Ultimately it took more than mere strength of arms to subdue it: the King's cause triumphed only through subterfuge and downright trickery. Carrying banners that depicted the five wounds of Christ, ancient symbols for traditional Catholic devotion, the rebels made sure that their demands were the focus of national attention. In the process, many found themselves caught in the unenviable position of being between a cause they espoused and a King they rightly feared.

John Neville was one such. Although his own sentiments were almost certainly allied with those of the Pilgrimage, he seems not to have been a man of particular courage or noteworthy intellect. Doubtless he hoped he might keep his head down at Snape and avoid entanglement. The pilgrims, however, had other ideas and, according to Latimer's version of events at least, kidnapped him at sword-point in order to dragoon him as a champion of their cause. As letters emerged from the rebel camp with Latimer's signature on them, whether written freely or under duress, his wife and children were left abandoned at home, in a hostile and unpredictable climate, to fend for themselves.

Worse was to come. As Latimer tried to disentangle himself from the mess into which he had either put himself or been placed by the violent threats of others, he moved south, towards London, in order to speak directly to the King and his advisers about the rebellion and its demands, as well as his own role within it. Back in Snape, 'rebel rebels', who saw the efforts to negotiate with the King as betrayal, invaded the castle and took Katherine and her stepchildren prisoner. We do not know what violence or humiliation they suffered, but the hostage-takers were brutal and ruthless: they demanded Latimer's return and threatened the life of his family. There was no question of their intent, and Latimer interrupted his progress southwards to dash home in fear. Somehow he persuaded them to release his wife and children unharmed, but the mental and emotional pressure on them all must have been enormous. Once again Katherine was left with huge responsibilities, no source of protection or help and meagre resources on which to draw. Once again it was her faith to which she turned, and to a prayerful spirit of trust and surrender amid the most trying, desolate and terrifying of circumstances. She later expressed this same spirit of resignation and hopeful commitment to God's providence in her published work as Queen:

> Lord, give me grace to suffer whatsoever thou wilt shall fall upon me, and patiently to take at thy hand good and bad, bitter and sweet, joy and sorrow; and for all things that shall befall unto me, heartily to thank thee.[44]

Katherine's hapless and inadequate husband somehow survived both his entanglements in the treason of the Pilgrimage of Grace and the consequent hostility and dislike of Thomas Cromwell, and returned home a chastened man. The price he paid for his weakness was to be forced to become Cromwell's emissary and enforcer in the north, required to undertake all manner of tedious and unpleasant tasks on behalf of his political masters. For three years this was the pattern of his life and, deprived of their London home by Cromwell's machinations, the Latimers remained mostly in Yorkshire. If their marriage was stable, it did not produce the children that presumably would have been expected. Nevertheless, their fortunes were raised somewhat by Cromwell's fall in 1540 and by the restoration of their home in the capital. As Latimer resumed his duties in the Lords, they spent more time there, and even as his life drew to its early end, Katherine's became unexpectedly enlivened by new company, new society, new possibilities – and the attentions of a monarch.

Certainly, for the kind of well-educated, highly intelligent and intellectually curious woman in her late twenties that Katherine was, London offered all sorts of interests and recreations that Yorkshire could not hope to rival. As her husband began to weaken, she went from strength to strength, certainly enjoying the company of like-minded and equally passionate gentlewomen who probably also encouraged her own increasingly reforming religious outlook. That is not to imply any lack of attention to or fondness for Lord Latimer, whom she nursed with commitment and careful attention until he died early in 1543, aged 50. As widowhood approached again, however, and as she was forced once again to take thought for herself and her young family in the lack of any male protector, she was introduced to two men whose influence on her, in different ways, would shape the rest of her life. They offered the hope not only of remaining in the city she had come to love but also of the security and the lasting love she also had long coveted.

Katherine, Lady Latimer, sought to exploit her mother's ties to the late Queen Katherine of Aragon by keeping the company of the Princess Mary, whom she may have known in childhood. Indeed, Queen Katherine had been Katherine Parr's godmother, in a strange irony of history. Whether there was a previous friendship or not, Katherine made sure to strike one up and soon became a member of the princess's retinue. Mary's own loneliness and emotional troubles were such that it was very likely that Katherine, with all her genuine powers of empathy, grace and wisdom, was a valued confidante and companion. So it was that she entered court life. And so it was that as her second marriage came to its close, which was fond if not passionate, she finally met the great passion of her life, the man with whom she first truly fell in love: Sir Thomas Seymour.

Everyone swooned at Thomas Seymour. He was handsome, dashing, passionate, colourful, exuberant and charming – when it suited him. He was also vain, often foolish, and overwhelmed with the taste for power. His sister's unexpected ascent to marriage to Henry VIII had given him and his brother Edward lofty ambitions, but only Edward had the brains and the capacity to realize them. In 1543 Thomas's return to court from a foreign embassy placed him in Katherine's company for the first time. Whatever happened between them and whatever motives were in play on either side, a real and lasting passion was kindled between them. Katherine was swept off her feet by Thomas's lusty sex appeal and witty company. Had matters not been complicated by the attentions of the King, it is certain they would have been married straight away. As it was, Katherine's own charms, intelligence and beauty made her an object of universal affection. And the claims of a King, couched in terms of duty to the realm itself, meant that his will had to be obeyed. Struggling to reconcile a genuine sense of her duty to her King with her newfound and heartfelt love for Thomas Seymour, she submitted to the royal demands, as she had to do. Seymour was sent away again to avoid rumour or scandal; and Katherine, the dowager Lady Latimer, became Queen Katherine, sixth and last wife to Henry VIII of England and Ireland, and stepmother to Prince Edward and to the princesses Mary and Elizabeth.

For all her other virtues, Queen Katherine never sought a life of monastic austerity and simplicity; as she made her home in the stately apartments of Hampton Court Palace, she certainly enjoyed the finer things of life: the latest fashions from continental Europe, lavish jewellery and even baths of goats' milk. As her wealth and fortunes grew, however, she never forgot those who relied on her generosity and kindness in the uncertain environment of sixteenth-century England, especially her stepchildren from her second marriage. Margaret came to court, indeed, to be close to her stepmother and continued to enjoy her protection, friendship and support. Nor can it have been all luxury and ease: by the time she married him, King Henry was in his early fifties, vastly overweight, plagued with recurring ulcers and gout and famed for his ill-temper and short fuse. The flaws in his character that his youthful virtues and talents had somewhat covered became all too painfully evident towards the end of his life: narcissistic and domineering, even for a king, he could brook no resistance and tolerate no disagreement. Anyone who sought to navigate the choppy waters of the late Henrician court – even the Queen – was taking their life into their hands every day.

Katherine, however, made a better job of being close to this tyrannical ruler than almost any of her contemporaries, and certainly better than her immediate predecessors as queen. In particular she worked hard, and with great patience, wisdom and insight, to heal the deep divisions within the royal family itself. Princess Mary was by this time a deeply wounded soul, the victim of her father's implacable animosity towards her mother and of his consequent vengeful fury towards Mary's own loyalty to her. Declared illegitimate by her father, Mary had been denied access to her mother in her last years because of Henry's cruel and spiteful rage. The princess Elizabeth, on the other hand, had never known her mother: Anne Boleyn was executed when her daughter was not yet three years old. Raised amid the chaos and confusion of her father's affections, Elizabeth was always vulnerable to the plots and schemes of others, and seems herself to have craved true companionship and kindness. In her new stepmother, well-read, vivacious, resourceful and compassionate, Elizabeth finally found the friend and mentor she longed for. Prince Edward, of course, was much better provided for than his half-sisters. The object of his doting father's joy and delight, he was prepared for kingship by scholars and tutors and never knew, as Mary and Elizabeth did, the waxing and waning of Henry's love. Nevertheless, the warmth of his correspondence with Katherine, even beneath the customary gentilities, suggests that for him too, a boy whose mother died through giving him life, her maternal kindness was a source of strength.

Thus it was that, with Katherine as Henry's wife, the Tudor family was as unified and as free of internal angst and hostility as it was ever to be. She soothed their woes; she calmed their fiery tempers; she reasoned gently towards reconciliation; she embodied the mature, sensible spirit their temperaments so needed. She also strove to embody the ideals of her faith and her intellect and to be an influential representative from within the ruling family for the values and priorities she most cherished. Katherine Parr was a Renaissance woman, and as Queen promoted humanist learning, England's connectedness with the rest of Europe in matters of the mind, and the kind of engaged and heartfelt commitment to Christianity the great figures of the age had modelled. Taking her cue from Erasmus' fierce advocacy of lay reading of Scripture, she did all she could to ensure that the Bible was accessible to those who could understand it; mirroring the spirit of Sir Thomas More, she was an ardent proponent of women's education, whose benefits she embodied herself, translating works from Latin and writing devotional works for publication. In this she echoed the sentiments of these humanist heroes, rather than those of Luther and his allies, in her call for the reform of the Church's life and practice. Even if she later became bolder in her expressions of Reformed Christian ideas, she exemplified in the early years of her reign the ideal of the new learning and of how it might be expressed in Henry's strange national Church.

Katherine the Queen was at the height of her powers, then, in the summer of 1544, and something about her vivacity, penetrating intelligence and wise good sense so impressed her husband that she was left as Regent of the realm during his excursion to France between July and September of that year, on a military campaign. Hostility to the rule of women, even as temporary regents, was great at this time: we should remember that England had not yet had a Queen Regnant, and would not do so for another nine years. Katherine of Aragon had been left as regent in similar circumstances 31 years earlier, but she was of royal blood and five years the King's senior. The appointment of Katherine Parr was therefore a bold one, but she repaid the King's trust, maintaining order, settling financial matters in the kingdom and holding her own among the jostling, ambitious courtiers with whom she had to do during this period.

As Henry grew older and his health continued to decline, the matter of the succession became an increasing preoccupation of those who surrounded the King and who hoped their own influence might be augmented after his death. There was no dispute, of course, that the boy Edward would be the new King, but he would, during his minority, require a ruling Council. The jockeying for place was necessarily covert but rarely subtle. Men at court sought prestige and power for themselves but also for their causes of various kinds, and none was more potent than religion. Henry's headship of the English Church had secured the nation's independence from Rome but it had by no means settled the character of national religious life. Conservatives at court, who were often in the ascendancy during these latter years of Henry's reign, were determined to maintain the Catholic stamp of the liturgy and practice of the Church of England; the Evangelicals were equally determined that Edward's coming reign should be one of continued reform, emphasizing what they saw as the clear teachings of the Bible and reflecting the 'pure' Christianity of the continental reformers.

Amid all these very male wranglings, one woman was a major factor. Her regency, which signified the King's admiration of her, along with her known sympathies towards the Evangelical cause, made the Queen a focus of both hope and suspicion. Nor was she, in all probability, neutral in the discussions, almost certainly hoping for a shaping role in the next reign, building on the good relationships she had with the royal children. She had already persuaded Henry to reinstate Mary and Elizabeth in his will and to reverse his cruel disinheritance of them: her opponents feared what else and further she might beguile him into adding. In all this subterfuge and machination, so characteristic at Henry's court because so encouraged by him, there is evidence that she became a target of some of the conservatives not long after her regency; but she was clever, and it was hard to find much on her. In 1546, however, amid the backlash against heresy that had caught Anne Askew up again in its ruthless pursuit, and in which Katherine herself was certainly meant to be a target, she was almost undone. Justifiably terrified, she escaped with her life, and her title, only through her customary pluck, resourcefulness and courage.

The most detailed version of the story of the plot against Henry's last Queen comes from John Foxe and is therefore to be treated carefully, although we know he took care to talk with those who were there. We may probably trust his assertion that it was, once again, Bishop Stephen Gardiner of Winchester who was the chief plotter: it fits his track record and his own – admittedly utterly sincere – priority of maintaining what he saw as 'true religion' in the realm. By 1546 Katherine had become less circumspect in her dealings with the King and with others; she had taken to arguing with Henry on religious matters; her espousal of some Evangelical and reforming causes was no secret; her allies at court and the members of her own retinue were very clearly of a 'Protestant' inclination. Gardiner and his associates seem to have hoped that they might trick the Queen and her ladies-in-waiting by a search of their property, in the hope of discovering banned, seditious, heretical literature. Indeed, their hopes were so high and their intelligence presumably so secure that they even managed to procure an arrest warrant for the Queen herself. The Spanish ambassador, always with an ear to the ground, reported home that a new royal wedding might be in the offing.

King Henry VIII was notoriously capricious in his opinions. His capacity venomously to turn on former friends and close confidantes needs no description. He could be especially ruthless in his treatment of his wives, as four of them could attest. Katherine learned of the extent of the plot against her, and had to act quickly. She knew that two things might save her that had been denied to others. The fact that Henry had real affection and admiration for her was vital, but this would be of no use in the face of the manipulation to which he had succumbed, unless she could actually be in his presence and plead her cause. Others, like Thomas More and Queen Anne Boleyn, died because their enemies made sure to keep them at a distance from the King and then were able to defame and destroy their character and intentions as they pleased. So having ordered any incriminating books to be well hidden, she took to her bed and claimed to be seriously and dangerously ill. The ruse worked, and an anxious King came to her bedside. Through the course of a difficult and sometimes angry conversation, she was able to persuade him of her loyalty and her love, and to make the rather unlikely claim, nevertheless swallowed by a King who seems genuinely to have wanted to find a reason to excuse her, that her arguments with him about religion were merely play, designed to keep his mind active and to distract him from his physical ailments. He was pacified. When the ever-eager Thomas Wriothesley, unaware of the reconciliation, came to arrest the Queen as she walked with Henry the following day, the King's outburst of fury was something to behold. Just as he had failed with Cranmer in 1543, so Gardiner failed now to bring down a Queen.

Nevertheless, when Henry did die just a few months later in January 1547, and although the Evangelicals at court were by then in the ascendancy again, Katherine was not included on the regency council for the boy king. With her life turned upside down again, the dowager Queen retreated once more to private life. She did maintain her friendships with her stepchildren, and especially with the Princess Elizabeth, to whom she was close in temperament, character, outlook and instinct. She was also reunited with an old flame: returning home from his foreign embassies, Thomas Seymour seemed every bit as dashing and desirable to her as he had four years earlier. So recently widowed, and still in the customary two-year period of mourning, she was technically no more free now than she had been in 1543 to marry him. Still, finally free, as she herself described it, after decades of following duty and being subject to the follies and foibles of successive husbands, Katherine at 35 years old gave in to what her contemporaries thought improper and scandalous. Faced with Seymour's ardent declarations of love – and lust – and longing herself to consummate a relationship she can hardly have forgotten in the intervening time, she began an affair. Just months after Henry's death, they married in secret. When their union became public they faced public scandal and the disapproval of their friends, the Princess Mary foremost among them. But Katherine hoped that, finally, she would find security, peace and genuine happiness after a lifetime of turmoil and danger.

Baron Seymour of Sudeley, as he soon became, was not, alas, the man to offer this stability to his new bride. Apart from anything else, he became increasingly preoccupied with the jealousy he felt towards his brother Edward, appointed the young King's Protector and thus infinitely more influential in the realm. Thomas's efforts to supplant his brother and increase his own role at court became increasingly toxic. Edward's wife Anne was herself a rather vain and self-important woman, and initiated a quarrel with Queen Katherine about the use of the jewels of the King's wife, to which she felt entitled as the wife of the King's Lord Protector. This was not a game of 'Happy Families'. Thomas's inability to settle down, and his incessant efforts to do better for himself, were not conducive to the settled life for which Katherine longed, after a vastly different kind of existence. In addition there was the very strange affair of their house guest, the Princess Elizabeth. Thomas's behaviour with her, including horseplay and tickling 'romps' in her bedchamber, went far beyond what should have been normal between a 14-year-old girl and her almost 40-year-old stepfather. Katherine at first refused to believe that anything was wrong and even encouraged the relationship, but eventually sent Elizabeth away. Seymour's interest in the princess after Katherine's death, and Elizabeth's apparently deep affection for him, point to a very complex situation indeed, from which Elizabeth was fortunate to escape. Katherine's own absolute devotion to her fourth husband seems to have blinded her to his intentions and to aspects of his character.

Still, it may have seemed that in one respect at least, Katherine's final marriage was going to crown her life with an unexpected and welcome blessing: a child. She became pregnant in late 1547. The pregnancy was a very late one for the time, and during its course Katherine was undergoing the trials and anxieties just described. Seeking some peace and rest towards its end, having sent Elizabeth away, she retired to Seymour's estate at Sudeley Castle in Gloucestershire. Her daughter Mary was born in August 1548. It soon became clear, however, that Katherine was not recovering as she should: fevered, rambling and clearly not in her right mind, her condition deteriorated rapidly. Thomas Seymour did his best to comfort and console his wife, of whom he was certainly immensely fond, but she died six days after Mary's birth. Thomas himself was to live only a few more months before execution for treason in March 1549, and the child almost certainly died aged two in the care of her foster mother's household. A succession of tragedies thus engulfed a family who had hoped for a vastly different kind of life and future, but whose own natural health and disposition, character flaws, and sheer bad luck ultimately overcame them.

This extraordinary, brilliant, devoted and shrewd Renaissance Queen has been rather lost to posterity. Her achievements were necessarily overshadowed by those of her stepdaughter Elizabeth, but Elizabeth herself was shaped and influenced by no one more than by her stepmother. There is so much, however, for which Katherine Parr ought to be remembered and universally admired. Tremendously courageous under the most desperate circumstances, resourceful and determined amid catastrophe and the failure and absence of the men in her life, deeply committed to advancing the cause of learning and piety, she left her mark on her age and, through those she nurtured, on the generation that followed it. But it was to her faith that she always turned in crises and insecurities, and it was her faith she wished the world most to remember of her after her death. Her *Prayers or Meditations*, published in 1545, already reflected the Augustinian sentiment that formed the constant longing of her heart, a desire, amid all the turbulence she continued to endure, to place her trust and hope where alone they could truly be safe:

> Nevertheless, it shall be better with me, when it shall please thee; for thou, O Lord, only, art he that mayest help me, and thou mayest so confirm and stablish me, that my heart shall not be changed from thee, but be surely fixed, and finally rest and be quieted in thee.[45]

The *Lamentation of a Sinner*, published in 1547, revealed the Queen's evolving reforming sentiments, and was theologically much more obviously Evangelical than its predecessor, which had been largely based on patterns of medieval devotion such as Thomas à Kempis' *Imitation of Christ*. More fascinating than that, though, was the way the *Lamentation* reflected her own meditations on royal power and on her experience of the court and high office. Written while she was Queen, not long after she acted as regent during a time of war, it becomes clear why she could not have published it while Henry lived:

> The princes of the world never did fight without the strength of the world: Christ contrarily went to war even against all the strength of the world. He fought, as David did with Goliath, unarmed of all human wisdom and policy, and without all worldly power and strength. Nevertheless, he was fully replenished and armed with the whole armour of the Spirit; and in this one battle he overcame for ever all his enemies. There was never so glorious a spoil, neither a more rich and noble, than Christ was upon the cross, who delivered all his elect from such a sharp and miserable captivity. He had in his

battle many stripes, yea, and lost his life, but his victory was so much the greater. Therefore, when I look upon the Son of God with a supernatural faith and light, so unarmed, naked, given up, and alone, with humility, patience, liberality, modesty, gentleness, and with all his other divine virtues, beating down to the ground all God's enemies, and making the soul of man so fair and beautiful; I am forced to say that his victory and triumph was marvellous; and therefore Christ well deserved to have this noble title, Jesus of Nazareth, King of the Jews.[46]

The *Lamentation* reveals how, for all her ability at courtly intrigue and power play, Katherine saw right through them both and had, as a result of lengthy, heartfelt and prayerful consideration, come to detest the 'self-love' of her world and the 'blind judges' around her, who assessed every situation and prized every alliance only in terms of what they could gain. Echoing her close confidant and friend, Archbishop Thomas Cranmer, whose own humility and modesty in personal advancement were similarly remarkable and yet whose determination to use his august office to advance the cause of the gospel was absolute, she remarked:

> I thank God, by his grace, I hate no creature – yea, I would say more, to give witness of my conscience, that neither life, honour, riches, neither whatsoever I possess here, which appertaineth to mine own private commodity, be it ever so dearly beloved of me, but most willingly and gladly I would leave it to win any man to Christ, of what degree, or sort soever he were.[47]

This kind of claim, sincere in its expression and rooted in the Queen's genuine conviction, reflects a wisdom and a perspective that were hard-won. It reflects also a faith that, beneath the divisions and theoretical theological arguments of the day, was equally sincere, and cultivated by Katherine with assiduous devotion because of the comfort and refuge it gave her amid continual change and successive perils. She went home to Sudeley in 1548, weary of masculine aggression, dismayed by religious violence and depressed by the constant, bitter rancour of sectarian strife, but yet still confident in her God and trusting in God's continued purposes in her life – and, if God willed it, in her death. As the opening line of her *Prayers or Meditations* had expressed it:

Most benign Lord Jesus, grant me thy grace, that it may always work in me, and persevere with me unto the end.

In that hope, at least, she was not disappointed.

5

'Nourished with Hope': Nicholas Harpsfield

No less than their Protestant neighbours, English Catholics during the Reformation experienced a dramatic roller-coaster experience of the rising and falling of their fortunes. Indeed, rarely have hopes been more cruelly dashed than when, after five years, Mary Tudor died in 1558, leaving her realm to her half-sister Elizabeth and making the English Church vulnerable to the return of Protestantism. For all, regardless of their religion, meeting the changes and chances of these kinds of fortunes, which must indeed have felt 'outrageous', proved a test of faith and character. The victory of Protestantism under Elizabeth, and its subsequent celebration by John Foxe and others in ways that have indelibly and grotesquely fixed the character of Catholicism in the English imagination, have sometimes obscured the real grief English Catholics were forced to undergo. It has also often blinded subsequent generations to the sincerity of their convictions, the determined nature of their actions and the passionate engagement of their energies in seeking to maintain the Catholic cause in a country they loved as much as the Evangelicals did.

For English Catholics who came to maturity during the last years of Henry VIII and then lived through the rapid progress towards radical Protestantism under Edward VI, before seeing Mary Tudor restore papal supremacy and Roman Catholic practice and Elizabeth finally remove both at a stroke, one figure from the recent past became iconic. Sir Thomas More, celebrated in life, acquired even greater celebrity status in death because to the next generation of English Catholics he embodied all that had been lost – and all they hoped might still be regained. He also embodied the wise foresight that had accurately predicted in the first place what a royal supremacy would mean: national division, widespread rebellion and a descent into apostasy. More's England was the envy of the world: erudite, pious, cultured, colourful, united and deeply connected to the rest of Christendom by ties of devotion and belief. English people then were citizens of the world and representatives of a proud Christian identity and tradition, held together by a shared allegiance to Rome. Thomas More, more than any other single figure, had fostered, nurtured, celebrated and incarnated these virtues. He stood for what Catholics felt they had lost. And he offered a vision of the self-confidence to which England could again return. He was a talisman for their hopes amid the grief of their losses.

The man who did more than anyone else to enable English Catholics to understand their debt to More and realize the dynamism of his legacy for their future plans was Nicholas Harpsfield. His *Life of More* was in fact one of the earliest examples of a biography in English. Later, a prisoner under Elizabeth, he undertook a much more ambitious project in which he sought to place saints like Thomas More within the widest possible context: the canvas of the whole of Church history. But the purpose was the same: to demonstrate to his fellow religionists the authenticity of their faith by proving its longevity and changeless witness to the nation over time. Harpsfield's publishing projects were expressions of the central aims and ambitions, first of the Marian regime itself and subsequently of the ongoing but increasingly diminishing dreams of the English Catholic community. His place in this collection, therefore, is to give us a glimpse into the experience of a group often vilified, usually misunderstood and yet no less deeply affected – indeed in some ways more so – by the events of the English Reformation.

The life of Nicholas Harpsfield also offers an intriguing glimpse into the experience of someone born into early Henrician England, and thus just beginning to be aware of public and religious affairs in the nation as some of the most momentous events of the reign were unfolding: born in the City of London in 1519, he would have been just 16 at the time of More's death, and it is inconceivable that a young man of his intellect, energy and ability – he was educated at Winchester School and New College, Oxford – would have been unaware of and unaffected by such events. Originally trained as a lawyer, we know little else of Harpsfield or of his early career. In 1550, however, we do know that he joined a group of Catholic exiles who fled to Louvain, modern Leuven in Belgium, a city with a prestigious Catholic university and a growing tradition of welcoming Roman Catholic refugees from the areas of Europe experiencing the increasing hegemony of Evangelical theology and forms of government. We may assume that by this time Harpsfield was ordained as a priest, and that the ordeals of such a relocation were preferable to continuing to serve in a Church whose theology he regarded as heretical. We may also assume that, as a scholar of promise, he made great use of Louvain's academic facilities and deep commitment to the old faith.

What we know about this sojourn in Belgium is that it brought him into contact with a man whose friendship became vital to his subsequent career. Antonio Bonvisi was one of Thomas More's closest and dearest friends, whose skills had been employed by Henry VIII and his government in financial affairs but who had also fled England under Edward and was living himself, although Italian by birth, in Louvain. He maintained contact with the family of his old friend. Harpsfield most likely became Bonvisi's house guest in exile. Through him the younger man learned tales of the former Lord Chancellor and of the great and momentous events that had surrounded both his career and service to the King, and his downfall. Through Bonvisi, too, Harpsfield came into contact with More's own family, and especially his son-in-law William Roper. He also met William Rastell, a man 11 years his senior, whose father's printing works had been responsible for the publication of some of More's works. Rastell had entered the family business, only to feel his conscience command him to join the Catholic exiles. Thus it was that, in Louvain, Harpsfield found himself in the middle of a small circle of More intimates, relations and champions. Their friendship left an indelible mark on him. It also suggested to him the kinds of resources, couched in the life story of their greatest and wisest hero, that English Catholics needed if they were ever to recover the soul of their country again.

Nicholas Harpsfield thus immersed himself in Louvain life and company, and in continued dedication to a life of learning and prayer. That exile community must have assumed that the future belonged to English Protestantism, with a boy King just approaching adolescence, a ruling Council that was solidly and increasingly Evangelical, and religious reforms that, by the early 1550s, were placing England at the forefront of the continent-wide Protestant advance. But they could take some comfort in the strength of their faith in some areas of Europe, and in the signs of Roman Catholic renewal that were beginning to emerge: the great new Ecumenical Council that Pope Paul III had finally launched in the Alpine city of Trent in 1545 began its second session under Pope Julius III in 1551. Although it was soon interrupted again by war, there was a new and growing confidence about the cause. Harpsfield and his peers had to trust that there would be some role for them in future, however bleak the prospects of the renewal of Catholic faith and practice in England appeared.

In the event, of course, the unexpected accession of Mary Tudor to the English throne in summer 1553, and the way the English people rose up to overthrow the usurper Lady Jane Grey and place Mary on her father's throne, were an extraordinary and miraculous surprise, which, to the English Catholic exiles and their co-religionists back home, seemed like the clearest sign of divine providence and purpose. Most of the exiles returned home immediately, determined to play their role in what seemed to them the glorious if arduous task of rebuilding England and re-instilling Catholic faith, Catholic devotion and Catholic practice into a national Church whose worship had been forcibly and dramatically altered by two books of Common Prayer in close succession. To those Catholics, the prayer books had severed English people's direct connection to God's life. It was therefore a clear and absolute priority to reconnect them: through the reintroduction of the Mass; the restoration of image and colour in worship; the renewal of a lively sense of the presence of the saints; and a fresh inculcation of the sense of the continuity between this life and the next. Underpinning all these tasks, too, and crucial for the success of their whole project, was the re-establishment of the Pope's supremacy in English religious matters and the abolition of the 20-year-old royal supremacy in England. Ironically, Mary initially had to use the royal supremacy to enact the measures needed to reconcile England to Rome, and hated having to do so. But her replacement for Cranmer as Archbishop of Canterbury, Cardinal Reginald Pole, returned from his own exile overseas, having fled the wrath of his cousin Henry VIII in 1532. After the lengthy legal and political delays attendant upon the project were overcome, Pole finally, as papal legate, offered a national absolution in November 1554. Now the rebuilding project could begin in earnest. A nation lured away from it had to return to Roman Catholic religion.

As Pole took over from Thomas Cranmer as Archbishop, Nicholas Harpsfield was appointed to assume the archdeaconry of Canterbury from Cranmer's brother Edmund. He thus assumed a position right at the heart of the English ecclesiastical establishment as Mary's project came into force. The Archdeacon of Canterbury traditionally represents the Archbishop at various events within the Province of Canterbury, including the enthronement of diocesan bishops, and exercises a particular role of oversight within the diocese itself, regulating and ensuring the efficacy of the lives of the churches within it. Harpsfield set about his task with energy and enthusiasm. The returns from his visitation of the parishes in his care reflect his eye for detail, his pastoral sensitivity and concern, the priority he gave to the restoration of colour, image and beauty to the churches' worship, and the serious sense of duty he brought to the task. Beyond the material fabric of the church buildings themselves, he adjudicated disputes, settled long-standing problems in the lives of these communities, regulated aspects of parish life that concerned him – including dealing with those accused of witchcraft – and sought to inculcate in the priests their own deep and sacred responsibility to the lives of their flock. These included the careful provision of regular worship, which brought those present right into the mystery and glory of God's presence and purpose in their lives.

Harpsfield's visitation of these parishes within his 'patch' has become a model of efficient church government. But we should not neglect to recognize them also as a touching example of his pastoral sensitivity and firm commitment to the spiritual lives of the people. His was a vision that reflected that of his hero Thomas More, of the need to instil interconnectedness among the worshipping community: to remind them of their continuing and life-giving connection to the saints; to forge a new sense of unity between and among Christians in all places, held together by the authority of the Pope and the universal celebration of the Mass; and above all to strengthen their sense of their connection to God, whose very life became present to them on the altar and whose presence was everywhere around them and revealed to them in holiness and devotion. Through his meticulous, rigorous and scrupulous endeavours, Harpsfield hoped to restore Catholicism and thus to restore the unity, charity and sanctity he felt England had rejected in its embrace of royal supremacy and isolated religious policy.

We gain, through studying visitations like Harpsfield's more carefully, a much better sense of Queen Mary's purpose and the effect of her religious policies. The burnings of Protestants have rather tended to dominate our sense of these five years, largely because John Foxe's commemoration of his martyrs has been so widely read and deeply influential. But as we will discover, religious violence did not stop on Mary's death in 1558; nor was it by any means solely the policy of Roman Catholics. John Calvin in Geneva in 1553 was all too willing to consent to the burning of the arch-heretic Michael Servetus, after all, and John Foxe himself, although of a more pacific frame of mind than most at the time, was sometimes heard to call for the execution of those whose views he deemed beyond the acceptable limit. Beneath Foxe's propaganda, though, we see a rather different picture. The restoration of the old religion under Mary was actually rather effective; it was very often extremely competently overseen; and it had at its heart not a brutal, bloodthirsty, flint-like spirit but a concern for the beauty of the sanctuary, the mending of wounds in communities and of disputes between individuals, and the reassuring of the faithful that God was with them. In many places, too, the faithful were in fact only too happy to have their old religion back, and only too grateful for the hope and confidence it gave them in unsettled times of the providence and grace of God.

From the perspective of Marian Catholics like Nicholas Harpsfield it wasn't hard to see how and when the rot in English religious life had set in. Henry VIII's divorce of Queen Katherine of Aragon had been an act of outrageous cruelty, hypocrisy and even heresy; his spurning of the Pope's authority had led directly to social breakdown, religious division, national apostasy and immorality. The truth was that the Erastian views of Cranmer and others had dangerous consequences: if the monarch was deemed the sole arbiter of Truth in all matters, without the need to refer to others, maintain consistency with his predecessors or uphold the unity of Christendom, then the highly individualized rule that followed would be entirely unpredictable and deeply problematic. Roman Catholics in England saw a succession of rebellions and protests in their land after the royal divorce: the Pilgrimage of Grace, Kett's rebellion, Wyatt's uprising and so on. They saw too the pace of religious reform under Edward VI accelerate alarmingly, such that by the end of it all trace of the Mass had gone, altars had been removed from English churches and all the vividness and dynamism of the old faith had literally been whitewashed away. And they concluded, naturally enough, that the royal supremacy was the problem. Henry's tastes in religious matters were rather conservative; but after his death the radically reforming views of the boy king and his council were given free reign. England had been left entirely exposed, adrift and unprotected, her national life and her very sense of herself subject to the whim of the monarch on any given day. As they set about repairing what they judged the appalling damage of what they inherited, they were therefore clear about the main culprits for the mess – and about the main hero who had correctly resisted their designs.

Late in Mary's reign, Nicholas Harpsfield was at the centre of a major publishing project, apparently with approval from Pole and even the Queen herself, to spell out for English people the causes of their condition and the virtues now revealed as imperative for their national renewal. The causes of the rot were embodied in two men: King Henry and Archbishop Cranmer. The virtues had been incarnate in Sir Thomas More, whose life, wisdom and death now became absolutely central to this official effort to remind England of the recent past and summon her people back to their true character. In 1557, William Rastell, who had returned from Louvain to take over the family printing business, published the first folio edition of the complete works of More, which the exiles among his circle had carefully preserved in their flight and treasured during the reign of Edward. To accompany this great literary event, Harpsfield himself composed two treatises, which were designed to place More and his thought, as well as the Marian religious restoration, in context: a biography of the man himself, and an account of the 'Pretended Divorce' between King Henry and Queen Katherine.

Harpsfield's *Life of More* had a fairly straightforward purpose: to remind the English of their great Renaissance man and in particular to emphasize his remarkable, prescient wisdom in resisting the divorce, which he rightly saw as destructive of unity, social cohesion and religious identity. It is a very touching portrait in some ways. Harpsfield describes More's learning and his friendship with Erasmus and great minds of contemporary Europe; he discusses More's own struggles with choosing between a monastic or a family life and recounts how there were always elements of the former that he maintained amid the reality of the latter: solitary Fridays spent alone in prayer in his library at Chelsea, and donning a surplice to sing with his church choir at weekends. Harpsfield outlines More's tender relationships with his nearest and dearest too: the account of his efforts to win his son-in-law William Roper back to the Catholic faith during his brief but intense flirtation with Lutheranism is particularly memorable and striking, and was in all probability a story that would have resonated with those for whom Harpsfield was writing, in the aftermath of two decades of rapid religious change. It was also an accurate and reliable account, drawing on first-hand knowledge and Harpsfield's friendship with Roper himself.

Despite such stirring descriptions of domestic matters, it is More's resistance to the King's divorce that naturally dominates the narrative. There are various 'bit-part' players: Cardinal Wolsey swaggers on to the scene early on, a man in Harpsfield's eyes so obsessed with his own advancement and personal power base that he is prepared to countenance any action and execute any strategy to satisfy his royal master. Like any king, Henry is surrounded by the usual compliant courtiers, all desperate to curry favour and secure their own position, whatever the cost to their conscience or their soul. But it is Henry himself who takes centre stage, and Harpsfield's portrayal of him spares nothing, even of so high-born a figure. It is tempting to see Queen Mary's own deep woundedness at the hands of her father being expressed through the pen of her own subject, as Harpsfield ruthlessly exposes the hypocrisy of Henry's position and the increasing cruelty of his treatment of his wife and daughter. Above all, misled by self-interested advisers, deceived by his own lust for power – and for Anne Boleyn – and duped by the Erastian solution to his problems, Henry sets his own opinion above the common consent of the Christian world, no matter what the cost to his realm. It is the resistance to this that makes More, for Harpsfield, England's saint and champion. At the height of the episode, Thomas Cranmer asks More why he will not obey Henry in the divorce, as he should. The reply is devastating:

> Sir Thomas More answered that he thought that was one of the causes in which he was bound not to obey his prince. And if that reason may conclude, then we have a way to avoid all perplexities: for in whatsoever matter the doctors [i.e. scholars] stand in great doubt, the King's commandment, given upon whether side he list [whatever side he wished], solved all the doubts.[48]

The apparently ludicrous nature and obvious tendency of the royal supremacy stand starkly revealed.

The nature of the divorce itself, and of Henry's motivations for it, are discussed at greater length in Harpsfield's *Treatise on the Pretended Divorce*. Although it is a less attractive book and a less easy read than the *Life of More*, it does assert a viewpoint on these events that many since have espoused, Catholic or Protestant. He takes very seriously the King's appalling treatment of Katherine, and of her daughter Mary by extension, questioning the character of a man who 'would disinherit her and dishonour himself as it were by open proclamation, declaring and proclaiming himself to all the world to have lived in grievous incest about twenty whole years'. Harpsfield adds that Henry's obsession with a male heir ended up producing one who led England into schism, whereas his eldest child, although female, has shown herself to be 'God's blessed minister' who has restored England 'to the unity of the Church that we had before abandoned'. Henry's lust for Anne Boleyn, he claims, was a sort of idolatry: blinded by it, slave to his own passion, the King sold his country down the river to satisfy his own desires. And once he had developed a taste for such casual marital affairs, he became insatiable, getting through four more wives before death brought an end to his reign. In all of this the

King's narcissism and absolute belief in the sacred truth of his own opinions spurred him on, now unbridled by the counsel of any minister or the wisdom of any courtier.

Like the intemperate, furious screeds of Thomas More and Martin Luther against one another, Nicholas Harpsfield's attacks on Thomas Cranmer in these treatises can sound strident and harsh to modern ears. Indeed, they are. In this Harpsfield reflects the Queen's own view again: her implacable hatred of the former Archbishop was visceral and absolute, leading her to execute him even after his apparent recantation of his Protestant views. Put simply, of course, she could never forgive him for his sanction of her mother's divorce from her father, and for his giving the necessary ecclesiastical blessing to the policy that declared her illegitimate, caused her mother's final years to be racked with misery and depression, and separated her from Katherine entirely, so that she was unable even to tend her as she died. Harpsfield came to his project in the immediate aftermath of Cranmer's death, and to counteract some of the fame it had won him. As we have already seen, Cranmer was no less complex and no less human than any of the players in this Tudor drama: capable of compromise that draws his judgement into question, as well as of courage that Foxe rightly celebrated later. For Harpsfield, and from the perspective of 1557, Cranmer's legacy did not have anything like the kind of lustre it does today. For his role in the divorce and in England's subsequent and rapid movement towards Reformed Christianity, he is thus savaged in these works.

Perhaps the most eye-catching and subsequently influential element of Harpsfield's assault on Cranmer was his attack on his secret marriage. For Protestants, as we have seen, Cranmer's devotion to Margarete was brave and praiseworthy, as he sought to be loyal to a wife whom he married apparently without any sense of his imminent and meteoric promotion. For Catholics, of course, the position looked far more compromising, as the Archbishop in office upheld a ban on clerical marriage even as he kept his own wife and children hidden at home. The measures required to maintain this secrecy amid the dangers of the Henrician court, Harpsfield made legendary with his story of Cranmer's special wooden box, drilled with holes, in which he transported his wife when travelling. Similarly, Cranmer's willingness to compromise with his own conscience in order to maintain his position draws fierce and not entirely unwarranted criticism. Having countenanced one divorce, he went on to sanction others, without even the flimsy pretext of the first one; he could at times be unwilling to acknowledge his own culpability in events; his views seemed to have evolved over time and at the last he gave them up altogether.

To modern ears the unfairness of some of these accusations is great. It is hard to deny that they are, for the most part, based on the truth, albeit often stretched and manipulated beyond recognition. Cranmer's defence, as we have seen, rested on the extraordinary circumstances in which he lived and his own absolute commitment to the cause of Evangelical religion in England. But commitment to that cause seemed a dreadful thing to Marian Catholics, especially those, like Harpsfield, with a leading role in the restoration of the ancient faith. To his fingertips the intellectual descendant of Thomas More, Harpsfield saw the unravelling of the stability and pride of the first 45 years of Tudor rule into the endless innovation, turmoil and upheaval of the period since 1532 as entirely the fault of religious change. And the prime movers of that change, King Henry and Archbishop Cranmer, had to bear the blame. In a Latin work designed to describe Cranmer's vacillation at the end of his life, Harpsfield catalogued the 'slaughter of good men . . . the ransacking of the Church . . . the massacre of the nobility . . . the oppression of the people' that he felt he had witnessed in England.[49] Towering above all his contemporaries in foresight, judgement, wisdom and statecraft, Thomas More reminded the English of what they had lost, and of the greatness, unity and connectedness to which they could again aspire as, under Mary Tudor, England rejoined Christendom and took her place once more among the nations.

These treatises, on the life of Thomas More, the initiation of the royal supremacy and the late hesitation of Thomas Cranmer about Protestant faith, were never published. Intended for a wide audience, to bolster the return to papal obedience and instil in English people a clear historical understanding and appreciation for More's wisdom in foreseeing the troubles that would come, they remained in manuscript. The main reason was that Mary Tudor herself died, aged 42, in November 1558. Their purpose thus became redundant, even as their author, seeing the inevitable consequences of the accession of Princess Elizabeth to the throne, tried to escape back to Louvain. It is instructive, however, to consider what important books they would have become had the Queen lived and produced Catholic heirs. As Catholicism was re-established as the bedrock of the nation's religion, and as things began to return to how they had always been, the brief reign of Edward VI would have been seen as an aberration in an otherwise uninterrupted and entirely continuous connection to the rest of the Christian world. The wisdom of Sir Thomas More, available in printed form for the literate public, and underpinned by the memory of his life, foresight and good judgement in the face of royal folly and pride, and of his self-sacrificial death, would have been for all time a reminder of what had so nearly been lost.

Such an achievement would have been great indeed. But the premature death of the Queen and the longevity of her successor made it impossible. As it was, Mary's reign was seized on by Protestant polemicists in the years following, who capitalized on her weaknesses and flaws as Harpsfield had sought to exploit Henry's and Cranmer's. She had been for ever and permanently damaged by her father's unspeakable cruelty to her and to her mother. Her marriage to Philip of Spain was ill-advised and deeply unpopular. She could be suspicious and untrusting, although her life and her circumstances gave her just cause. And as we have seen in the case of Cranmer, she could cherish resentments that were ferocious in their intent and implacable in their intensity. Further, when it came to eradicating the Protestantism she so loathed, both for its personal and for its national effects, Cranmer was far – very far – from being the only target of her rage.

So it was that in the hands of Foxe and others, not just Mary's but Roman Catholic character itself became fixed in the English imagination as cruel and persecuting, and the abiding symbol of these years is that of the brutal public execution by burning of around 280 Protestants. But once again we need, without excusing this kind of appalling violence and human cruelty, to keep a sense of perspective and, as has been described before and will be elaborated again in later chapters, recall the world in which these things took place, a world in which almost everyone approved of death for certain crimes, including heresy, and one in which modern understandings of religious tolerance were quite unknown: just read Luther's late diatribes against the Jews. Beneath the headlines of subsequent propaganda, however, and under the examination of more recent historical scholarship, the achievements of Mary's brief reign look rather more significant. There is every sign that, by 1558, England was re-embracing the old faith, not merely grudgingly but with growing enthusiasm, especially as the more ardent Protestants fled abroad themselves. Specifically English resources and virtues were deployed to strengthen the case for Catholicism, incarnated in Lord Chancellor More. Men like Nicholas Harpsfield had laboured with energy, insight, sensitivity and care to bring this about, and their achievements were real. If Mary had lived, they would have been critical.

The real test of Harpsfield's own character was just beginning, however. His effort to escape failed, and given his obdurate resistance to any imposition of Protestantism on the English Church, he soon found himself imprisoned. Except for a very brief period at the end of his life, he remained there until his death in 1575. Despite the loss of his hopes, the reversal of his achievements and the privation of his circumstances, Harpsfield set about a new project that was designed to be a contribution to the contemporary historical debates about the nature and character of the various Reformation disputes. The background against which he wrote was twofold: in Europe the so-called 'Centuriators' of Magdeburg were setting about a painstaking survey of Christian history, in which they sought to identify the heralds of 'true' Evangelical faith in every time and place, those who bravely took on the excesses of Roman Catholic teaching and practice and who lived, and often died, for their understanding of scriptural Christianity. In England, Elizabeth's Church of England needed to defend its own place in the Church Universal, and figures like Bishop John Jewel of Salisbury, and later John Foxe, sought to give it that credibility by a very similar method, attempting to chart its continuity with faithful Christians of all times, in particular through its affinity with the early Church. Thus, two very distinct approaches arose to Christian history: the Protestant version asserted authenticity through similarity with early Christianity, the so-called patristic age, and identified the upholders of this faith amid papal corruption and Catholic distortion in every generation since. Catholic historians, on the other hand, generally looked to continuity to prove their claims to truth. Under the guidance of the Holy Spirit and the papal supremacy, the Church had evolved over the centuries but in ways faithful to its Lord and necessary for its growth and mission. It was the heretics in every generation who endangered both.

Nicholas Harpsfield turned again to his hero in beginning to construct his own contribution to this debate. Thomas More had famously couched his own philosophical and polemical writing in the form of dialogues between two imaginary characters: this was, of course, the model of Plato and of the ancient world generally, whose spirit and wisdom humanists like More longed to emulate. Written in Latin to guarantee a wide continental readership, Harpsfield's *Dialogi Sex* ('Six Dialogues') were between Irenaeus, the champion of Catholic orthodoxy (named for the second-century theologian and Bishop of Lyons), and a German Protestant called Critobolus. First published in 1566 in Antwerp under a pseudonym, they were a vast survey of a whole range of issues at stake and argued over in the Reformation era. Deploying an extraordinary range and depth of knowledge, the dialogues methodically and exhaustively tried to reassure Catholics in general and English Catholics in particular of their direct and vibrant connectedness to God through the sacraments of the Church and the patterns of Catholic devotion inherited from the past. Harpsfield's hope was that the fictional conversations in the book might inform the conversations, actual and internal, of Elizabethans about their religion, demonstrate to them the power of the claims of Catholicism and restore them to their former faith. In discussions on the Mass, iconography as an aid to prayer, the lives and continued intercessions of the saints, the papacy as guarantor of authenticity and connector to Christ himself, and the true nature of priesthood and monasticism, his aim was to hold before his readers the dynamic nature of the Catholic Church and its channels of grace. He hoped thus to expose what he saw as the fearsome teaching of Protestantism, which taught its followers to trust their reason and ignore the witness of the Church to the power of God at work in material things, supremely bread and wine.

There was another main purpose in the dialogues, and one that was, partly at least, successful. In 1563 the first English edition of John Foxe's *Acts and Monuments* was published, and became an instant sensation. We have already examined its intent and method: the systematic exposure of the cruelty of Catholicism, in every time and place, when faced with the courage of Evangelicals of various kinds, standing on the word of Scripture and resisting papal error and Catholic innovation. Like Harpsfield's dialogues, Foxe's work was also vast in its scope. But it also contained errors of fact, which were demonstrable. Thus, as he set about his labour of love, Harpsfield devoted the last and longest of the dialogues to the repudiation of Foxe's work. In a sometimes dazzling display of learning he explored the internal divisions within Protestantism, particularly on the meaning of the Eucharist, the difficulties of the rather complex life and behaviour of Martin Luther and the seeming hypocrisy with which Foxe on the one hand rejected the Church's traditional martyr-saints and then on the other replaced them with less glorious ones of his own devising, or on the one hand scorned claims for the supernatural in Catholic teaching while on the other claiming visions and miracles for his own subjects. He also questioned the actual virtues of many of those Foxe held up as saints. When, in 1570, Foxe responded with a mixture of righteous indignation and some material changes to stories and interpretations that the dialogues had disproved, Harpsfield certainly felt his work had not been wasted.

Somehow Harpsfield managed to keep writing volumes of the same kind of historical material, dealing with the history of the English Church and with the nature of heresy in the land, focusing on John Wycliffe. The tenacity and courage this must have taken were enormous. After his death in 1575, subsequent generations of English Catholic writers and priests, in very different situations, found in his writings the resources they needed to inform their own understanding of their mission and to keep their own hopes alive. Above all, Harpsfield's great and continuing legacy was to hold the example of Thomas More aloft as the guiding light of what wisdom and courage looked like, and of the obligations all people ought to have, even above obedience to their governing authorities. In a small and less celebrated way he was another example of that brave persistence, whatever we think of his theological perspective or his political commitments. Although poised, by 1558, for a glittering ecclesiastical career that would probably have included episcopal office or a theological position, he was instead to spend the last 16 years of his life incarcerated. And yet there is no note of self-pity in any of his prodigious writings, only a deep love for his faith, the old faith of England, an abiding commitment to the principles and insights of his beloved Thomas More and a fervent, prayerful hope that the unity England once enjoyed with all the known Christian world might again be restored. Some might be surprised to learn that, in his view, love was indeed the supreme virtue, and it was for the restoration of the love that alone fosters human unity that he longed. As he said in the sixth dialogue:

> If we remain in Love – and Love alone – we shall never be able to leave the right path; or, if perchance some human failing should surprise us, it will be overcome by Love, like water by fire.[50]

6

The Virtue of Moderation: Matthew Parker

Sir, your signification uttered to me at my first coming to you at London, concerning a certain office ye named to me, did hold me in such carefulness all my time of being there ... [that it] made me to have so little joy of my being at London, as I had never less in my life; most glad when my back was turned thereunto. But, to come nigher to my intent of writing, I shall pray to God ye bestow that office well; ye shall need care the less for the residue. God grant it chanceth neither on arrogant man, nor on fainthearted man, nor on covetous man. The first shall sit in his own light, and shall discourage his fellows to join with him in unity of doctrine, which must be their whole strength; for if any heart-burning be betwixt them, if private quarrels stirred abroad be brought home, and so shall shiver them asunder, it may chance to have that success which I fear in the conclusion will follow. The second man should be too weak to commune with adversaries, who would be the stouter upon his pusillanimity. The third man not worth his bread, profitable for no estate in any Christian commonwealth, to serve it rightly.[51]

Thus wrote Dr Matthew Parker to his old friend Nicholas Bacon, the newly appointed Lord Keeper of the Great Seal under the young Queen Elizabeth, in March 1559. There is no false modesty here, no mock pretence of wishing to avoid promotion and preferment. The office in question was the Archbishopric of Canterbury; and Parker, told his name was in the frame for this crucial but impossibly difficult assignment, and foreseeing the struggles ahead for the soul and character of England's Church, did all he could to avoid it. Already in his mid-50s, a Cambridge man to his fingertips, he loved his life as a scholar and hoped, after the turmoil of the Marian years, to settle there and enjoy an academic life in retirement. He also – apparently quite genuinely – thought himself ill-equipped for a job he knew would be all-consuming, fearsomely intense and utterly thankless.

Bacon, William Cecil and the Queen herself agreed with Parker's description of the character needed by the new Archbishop, the successor to Reginald Pole, who had conveniently died on the same day as Mary Tudor. They knew that the task ahead was arduous and that the qualities most needed would be un-showy ones: tenacity, firmness of purpose, moderation and yet also a steely determination to see things through and impose common discipline on a divided Church. They agreed, putting a positive gloss on Parker's description, that the new Archbishop would have to be equanimous, courageous and selfless. Where they did not agree was on the extent to which Parker himself embodied the virtues they were seeking. Writing back to Parker just on the eve of his confirmation as Archbishop, Bacon observed:

> If I knew a man to whom the description made in the beginning of your letter might more justly be referred than to yourself, I would prefer him before you; but knowing none so meet, indeed I take it to be my duty to prefer you before all others, and the rather also because otherwise I should not follow the advice of your own letter.[52]

Matthew Parker's efforts to prove his unworthiness for the office had only proved his rightness for the times. He was duly consecrated in August 1559.

It's perhaps clear, with the benefit of hindsight, that Parker was attempting to fight the inevitable in seeking to resist his appointment to Canterbury. Apart from anything else, he had a deep emotional attachment to the Queen, and she to him. Parker had served as chaplain to her mother, Anne Boleyn, who seems to have been especially fond and trusting of this young clergyman. Even as he sought to avoid promotion, Parker was still remembering that, just days before her arrest, and as her enemies finally closed in on her, Queen Anne had entrusted her young daughter to his care and protection. Through her patronage, too, he had begun his ecclesiastical career, making a name for himself as a shrewd administrator, a keen academic and a man of absolute integrity and moral fibre. But the bond with Elizabeth went even deeper: like her, he had chosen to stay in England under the reign of Queen Mary, although doing so had meant the deprivation of all his income, his livings, his offices and his rank and privilege. Reduced to penury, Parker had hidden in plain sight for five years, even while around him his peers and co-religionists either found themselves arrested and tried or fled the country altogether, seeking the safety, and the purity of doctrine, of Strasbourg, Geneva, Frankfurt and Zurich. Like Elizabeth, therefore, Matthew Parker, having lived through all of England's recent upheavals and persecutions, understood its consequent need for stability, peace and unity. And the privations and dangers of Queen Mary's reign had surely forged a similar courage and insight in his soul as they had in hers.

Although his story is inextricably bound up with Elizabeth's, it is on Parker that we will focus first, before turning to his Queen, who consumes so much of the oxygen in any survey of Tudor England. For Matthew Parker is one of those extraordinary historical figures whose lack of flashiness or show was the very virtue by which he was able to achieve so much. A brilliant but quiet scholar, a husband and father who infinitely preferred his hearth and his family to royal palaces and ceremonial state occasions, a man gifted in administration but rarely one for grand gestures, Parker's groundedness and shrewd and careful observation were the Church of England's greatest assets in a period that could easily have been chaotic and even blood-soaked. Under his leadership, inclusion and moderation became not merely the marks of an imperfect compromise by which alone things could hold together but the essential DNA of a national Church whose very identity, forged amid religious division and violence, would come to uphold such an approach as the very heart of the Christian gospel itself. They are virtues the global Anglican Communion has never needed so urgently to recover and remember.

Matthew Parker, rather like More and Cranmer, was born into an age rich with the promise of future growth. Norwich in 1504 was a significant city and was his home until he moved to Cambridge as a student in 1522. He was not from a noble or important family but it seems that the stability and security of his upbringing left their mark on him and that the warmth of a happy family life was something he always subsequently coveted. The death of his father in 1516 must have been a terrible blow; but his mother remarried quickly, and under the tutelage of his various schoolmasters the boy Matthew made good progress and showed great promise. He arrived at Corpus Christi College eager to continue learning but little realizing how great a role he was going to play in this ancient university in the future, nor how much of a mark he would leave, both on its scholarship and on its administration.

Like the two Thomases, Parker found the world he had known and in which he had been formed radically rearranged; in his case, during his young adulthood. Along with Cranmer, his senior by 15 years but whom he probably knew in Cambridge, his own fortunes were about to be greatly improved, and the course of his future life set, by Henry VIII's marriage to Anne Boleyn. Already ordained priest and by then entering on a promising academic career as a fellow of Corpus, Parker was appointed one of Anne's chaplains in March of 1535, having caught the eye of reforming figures in Cambridge and impressed those around the new Queen as exactly the kind of 'bright young thing' who might serve her well. Anne evidently liked the young priest very much, securing for him an appointment to the prestigious Stoke-by-Clare College as its Dean. Stoke was the reshaped survivor of a medieval monastic institution, which had become a centre of learning and a coveted prize, especially for intellectual clergy like Parker. Here he whetted his appetite for academic administration, building on the College's illustrious past and reputation for the life of the mind in the service of the Church. As the Queen's chaplain he was also her confidant and adviser, albeit only briefly. So it was that, as already described, he was charged with a particular duty of care for the Princess Elizabeth by her mother, even as Anne's fate closed in on her. Parker could have had little idea about the manner in which he would ultimately serve and protect the small and vulnerable child he then knew.

Anne Boleyn's fall from grace – and power – did not dent Parker's own rise too much. Those around the King continued to value him and to rate his ability and his usefulness, such that the 1540s were in fact a period in which he continued his apparently smooth rise to prominence. He joined the ranks of the King's chaplains in 1537 and continued to amass various livings and preferments, as was common for the time: Ashen in Essex; Burlingham in Norfolk; Landbeach in Cambridgeshire; and a prebendal stall at Ely Cathedral. In 1544 he gained what for him must have been the prize he most desired when, through the commendation and choice of the King himself, he became Master of his old college, Corpus Christi in Cambridge. Henry's letter to the fellows of Corpus emphasized the new Master's 'approved learning, wisdom, and honesty' as well as his 'singular grace and industry in bringing up youth in virtue and learning' as the qualities that made him an obvious candidate for the job.[53] He was duly elected and embarked upon the duties of Master, a job that probably afforded him the greatest pleasure and fulfilment of anything he undertook, excepting his marriage and family.

So admirably did Parker take up the Master's duties at Corpus that he was twice, in 1545 and 1548, elected to the annual role of Vice Chancellor of the University. The execution of this role brought him into the line of fire of the University Chancellor, Bishop Stephen Gardiner of Winchester (later Queen Mary's

Lord Chancellor). The correspondence between him and Parker in 1545 is a fascinating glimpse, both into the reforming spirit of the University and into the tensions in religion at the highest levels of Henry's regime. Gardiner, as we have seen, whether through real conviction or expediency, became a firm supporter of the royal supremacy but maintained a fierce conservative line in religious matters. His keen eye for detail and his sometimes ferocious concern for what he saw as religious orthodoxy were a potent combination. Parker dealt with both with courteous inaction and masterly guile.

The incident at the root of their correspondence was a play. Christ's College students, with the consent of and even a small bursary from the college authorities, had staged a production of *Pammachius*, a third-rate drama otherwise best forgotten. With the radical, mischievous edge of undergraduates, the students deliberately chose provocative subject matter: the play contained some fierce critique of papal authority but also of traditional religious practices, including fasting and the cult of the saints. It was also, in places, rather crude and a little risqué. The budding thespians of Christ's were thus not so very different from their modern descendants: they desired their production to amuse, to cause a little scandal by making their elders uncomfortable and to offer a little satire on some of the hypocrisies and idiocies of contemporary life. Those used to dealing with undergraduates, with the wisdom of experience and the equanimity of having seen it all before, indulged their young charges.

Bishop Gardiner was not so wise. Informed by a Cambridge-based spy, he wrote to Parker, pompously inserting himself as Chancellor into the situation and demanding satisfaction about what exactly had been said and performed. Nor was he satisfied with Parker's initial reply, assuring him that no one was offended, except Gardiner's own informant, whose identity he had swiftly discovered, and advising him to busy himself with more pressing matters. Gardiner persisted, requiring Parker, in his name, to gather and reprimand senior members of the university and in particular those responsible for giving permission for the play's performance. Parker did so, we must imagine rather gently, and his second letter to Gardiner breathes a delightful air of both insouciance and placatory calm in the face of the Bishop's swagger, bluster and outrage. Still not satisfied, Gardiner instructed the Council to order the Vice Chancellor to continue his investigations and toughen his discipline: after a perfunctory letter from them to him, Parker seems to have let the matter drop altogether, with no further repercussions. The whole episode is fascinatingly revealing: along the way, Parker describes his own efforts to reconcile and reunify dissenting factions within Cambridge, a task later to be so central to his ministry as Archbishop. Throughout his dealings with the importunate Gardiner, Parker's surface poise and calm belie nerves of steel, a determination not to be pushed beyond what he considers reasonable, and a deep and humane commitment to the welfare of his university and its students, doing what all students have always done, in thumbing their nose at establishment and authority.

Parker remained in Cambridge for almost all of the reign of Edward VI, a time in which his own reforming views and those of the city itself were much more in line with official government policy. Indeed, Thomas Cranmer's efforts to link England's now-untrammelled Reformation to that of continental Europe had included the appointment of Martin Bucer to the Regius Chair of Divinity; Bucer valued Parker's friendship and appointed him executor of his will, a task Parker was forced to undertake when Bucer died in 1551. Parker had married Margaret, also from Norfolk, in 1547, slightly before mandatory clerical celibacy was officially overturned but after an already too-long engagement neither party could bear to prolong any further. They had three sons, born in 1548, 1550 and 1551,[54] two of whom survived into adulthood. His life at this time was all he wished for it to be: he was blessed with happiness at home and real fulfilment in his vocation, and rejoiced in the progress of scholarship in Cambridge and Evangelical Christianity in England. Only at the end of the reign did Parker's life change, when his ally the Duke of Northumberland installed him as Dean of Lincoln and he and his family travelled north to assume responsibility for one of England's largest, loveliest and most historic churches.

No sooner had Parker settled into the Deanery, however, than the greatest change of all crashed down on him and all those who had hoped that Edward's reign would usher in a long period of religious reform and renewal. Mary's accession to the throne left senior clergy like Parker, known allies of Northumberland and with clear commitments to the Evangelical cause, with a stark choice. Largely because of his family, perhaps, Parker decided against flight. While his friends and allies sought passage to continental Europe and to places where they could imbibe Protestant thought and practice in their purest form, he stayed in England. The consequences of this, for his later attitude and approach, were probably significant, as we shall see. But we should not imagine that the years of Mary's reign were entirely unpleasant to him. Mary's councillors moved swiftly to deprive of office all married clergy, and especially those as prominent and senior as Parker. Yet despite the great loss of income, rank, honour and status, and in the face of the danger of arrest and prosecution, Matthew Parker nevertheless came to see these as blessed years, no less the gift of divine providence – and indeed perhaps rather more so – than years of promotion, earthly honour and ecclesiastical authority. This essentially quiet, bookish, family man found himself able to indulge his greatest pleasures. As he described it himself:

> I lived as a private individual, so happy before God in my conscience, and so far from being either ashamed or dejected, that the delightful literary leisure to which the good providence of God recalled me yielded me much greater and more solid enjoyments, than my former busy and dangerous kind of life had ever afforded me.[55]

Accompanied by his 'good and virtuous wife' and his 'very dear children' he bided his time, trusting in the God who had provided for him thus far and hoping simply to be allowed to care for his family and attend to his research, even amid such straitened circumstances. These are the 'hidden' years of Matthew Parker: years in which his heart seems to have found its rest, in family and intellectual pursuit, and in which he did not crave the restoration of the 'dangerous' life of public office he had lost. When Mary died in November 1558, however, he must have known that his generally pleasant exile was coming to its end, even if he dreaded the prospect. Thus our story returns to where we began and to the young Queen Elizabeth's urgent search for a new Archbishop, a man who possessed the gifts necessary to guide the Church in England through yet another period of turmoil and change, towards what she hoped would be a period of stability and growth, and a new national unity of purpose.

The Elizabethan Settlement in religion has exercised generations of scholars, who have produced libraries of books about it, and is still a contested area of examination and interpretation among those who seek to discover more of its circumstances and in particular the intentions of the remarkable young woman behind it. Of that we will have more to say in the next chapter. For now we should remember that the Settlement was a compromise – for most anyway – and that it was viewed quite differently by many of those it affected. In the first place, the nature of the 'compromise' ought to be made clear: the Church of England was not designed to be a halfway house between Roman Catholicism and the radical 'fringe' of the Reformation. Instead it was designed to create, and doctrinally define, a firmly Protestant Church that, while allowing for some variety of thought and belief among its members, nevertheless resisted and rejected both the 'extremes': of a Catholicism under papal supremacy and retaining much medieval practice; and of the seemingly anarchic and dangerously radical Anabaptist movement.

Beyond that, there was all to play for. And the central, indissoluble tension at the heart of the Elizabethan Church, the most intractable problem with which Parker had to deal with as Archbishop, was this widespread sense that the Settlement of 1559 was merely a stopgap, a patch on the wound until a 'more excellent', more Reformed way could be pursued in English religion. For Elizabeth, however, the Settlement was not only the first but also the last word. Thus she found herself at odds with the majority of her clergy, who saw it differently: as a vastly imperfect solution in constant and urgent need of further reform. Many of them, we must remember, unlike the Archbishop, had spent the Marian years in the great centres of European Reformed Christianity; they had seen pure gospel faith, lived out and implemented in towns and cities across the continent; they had heard the sermons and enjoyed the conversations of the fountainheads of Protestantism in the places of its mature flourishing. They remembered Cranmer's vision of a Reformed English Church taking its full and proud place among the fellowship of such national churches. They longed for the completion of the trajectory on which, by 1553, England had been launched. They had returned home in 1558 full of hope. If the nature of the settlement disappointed them, many recognized the tough political situation in which the Queen and her ministers were operating, and hoped for better and greater things once firmer ground was beneath their feet.

They never came. As the years passed it became abundantly clear that what had been written in 1559 was unalterable, at least in the Queen's mind. Those like Parker who had not fled England or who simply adopted a more moderate view of things, argued for the 'middle way' of the Settlement, even if they themselves might have preferred a stronger outcome. The consequent tension, frustration, disappointment and resentment among the clergy, including many bishops, was a source of continual friction, private argument and public dispute for the rest of the reign and beyond. Among those areas the 'precisians' – who demanded further reform – generally criticized were: the retention of the episcopacy in a supposedly 'reformed' Church; the use of clerical vestments from the medieval past; the failure to eliminate 'superstitious' elements from worship, such as the sign of the cross in baptism or the use of the ring at weddings; and anything that compromised the Bible's stern warnings against idolatry, such as images in churches, certain kinds of music in worship and the Queen's notorious fondness for the crucifix. Try as they might, however, they were unable to win much concession on any of these points. As Parker's time as Archbishop progressed, he found himself faced with the endless task of requiring and enforcing conformity, even as English people increasingly identified with one or another party within the Church.

Matthew Parker, however, was not a moderate merely out of a sense of convenience, still less out of cowardice. His own preferences might well have been for a more thoroughgoing Reformation in England, but he attempted to enforce the Settlement with a consistency and a vigour, even to the end of his life, that must be admired. The Queen and he shared a determination to avoid the kinds of inquisitions and punitive interrogations on spiritual matters that had plagued Europe for centuries. Amid division they sought to create a truly national Church in which doctrinal declarations were broad enough to encompass a range of views, and breadth of personal commitment could be maintained amid the cycle of worship and the bonds of peace. To that end the Articles of Religion of the 1563 Convocation were deliberately few, tolerant and comparatively scaled down, both by comparison with the 1553 Articles but especially with the kinds of treatise-length catechisms and formulations of continental Europe. Conformity to the Church of England and to its liturgical life could still allow for a range of private convictions about faith; and Elizabeth and Parker were famously determined not to open windows on to the souls of the faithful in order to discover their inmost secret beliefs. There were certainly senior clergy who wanted greater rigour in this, some of whom advocated measures that would have made the Marian period look very tame. Out of a clear sense of what would, finally, make for stability in the realm, Parker fiercely resisted their efforts, despite the very personal ways he found himself under attack as a result.

Among the bishops, at least, he was able to forge some kind of unity amid the storm of the surrounding Church. Some of the more radical among them, who had pushed and manoeuvred for a more comprehensive Settlement, came to realize both that Parker's approach was the wise one and that they, and their cause, had far more to lose than gain by subverting and undermining the whole of the English ecclesiastical establishment. Perhaps, more cynically, the perks and privileges of being a diocesan bishop also worked their helpful effects. Nevertheless, the bishops' bench eventually stood firm and almost entirely united against the continued onslaught of the more radical wing and the non-conformists. They did so despite real divisions and disagreements among them on matters of faith and practice, but with a genuine commitment to the renewal of the Church of England. In all this, Parker's own generosity towards those with whom he disagreed, willingness to act as reconciler, and fierce loyalty to them all must have helped.

One of those whose views were initially rather different than Parker's was John Jewel, appointed Bishop of Salisbury on Elizabeth's accession. Jewel had spent time in the great bastions of Reformed thought, Frankfurt, Strasbourg and Zurich, and had been formed by their experience. Initially disappointed by the lack of progress in Elizabethan England, and temperamentally rather more explosive than his Archbishop, Jewel moderated his attitude and was employed as the greatest literary defender of the new Church. His *Apology of the Church of England*, first published in 1562, sought to lay out the biblical and early Church authority by which England's Church is constituted and from which it draws its own sense of authenticity. He challenged his Roman Catholic detractors to offer objections to his approach, and subsequently rebutted their arguments too, in a series of further writings throughout the 1560s. Jewel's work laid the foundations for all subsequent ecclesiology of the Church of England, and especially for the greatest apologist of Anglicanism of all, Richard Hooker, who was Jewel's pupil and protégé.

While in Frankfurt, Jewel had been a friend and associate of Richard Cox, who came to dominate the religious life of that city's exile community by successfully leading the resistance to the strong Calvinism of John Knox, later so influential in Scotland's Reformation. Cox, too, was known for his fiery temper and ruthless streak; but he also became one of Parker's most loyal lieutenants and reliable associates, responding to the Archbishop's persuasive leadership with affection and support. Cox was appointed Bishop of Ely in 1559, and he and Parker, so remarkably different in temperament, became friends and even in-laws when John Parker married Cox's daughter Joanna in 1566. Cox's role during the 1560s, and the letters between him and Parker, reveal the extent to which the Archbishop was able to forge a spirit of unity, strength of purpose and real affection among such a diverse group. This sense of common endeavour and mutual respect amid difference was absolutely crucial in these testing years, and Parker deserves enormous credit for his steady, humane and shrewd approach.

He also deserves a great deal of credit, as well as sympathy and commiseration, for his dealings with a Queen who, although they agreed on so much, often treated him with contempt and shameful disdain. Their respect for one another, not to mention the deep ties of affection and loyalty that went right back to Elizabeth's infancy, were real enough. And Parker's admiration for the way she had carried herself through her own trials and terrors, and then set her hand to the task of rebuilding the nation, was similarly heartfelt and long lasting. For all that, he endured much – from the relatively trivial to the culpably disgraceful. Nearer the former end of the spectrum was Elizabeth's rather old-fashioned dislike of married clergy. She had chosen Parker for Canterbury knowing that Margaret and his children would follow, and she realized that to legislate against the marriage of the clergy would be an impossible proposition. And so it became one of the things she 'winked at', despite disliking it with all her heart. Famously, after a visit to Lambeth Palace, the Queen is said to have taken her leave of her hostess with the extraordinarily graceless comment: 'Madam I may not call you; mistress I am ashamed to call you; so I know not what to call you; but yet I thank you.'

Far more severe and utterly more trying than this for Parker were the events surrounding the publication of the 'Advertisements' of 1566. Once again clerical clothing was at the heart of the furore. Those desiring a more deep-rooted and effective Reformation in England were furious at the mandate in the Elizabethan Church for clergy to continue to wear vestments that seemed to them vestiges of a papal past: copes at communion in particular, but also caps, surplices and tippets (a sort of preaching scarf). Such men preferred the simple clerical fashions of continental Europe, mainly consisting of gowns, and some were prepared to lose their livings and their appointments rather than collude in something they viewed as a fatal compromise with a devilish past. Many of the leading establishment figures, in trying to help such non-conformists find a way through, wrote letters to leading European reformers, including the great and universally admired reformer of Zurich, Heinrich Bullinger, who helpfully explained why, in his thought, such matters were 'indifferent' and not at all deleterious to England's Christian character. But such efforts were only of limited effect. Eventually the Queen's patience with the recalcitrant rebels ran out.

She directed her anger at poor Matthew Parker. In a long letter of early 1565 she poured out to him her anger and mounting frustration at the 'diversity, variety, contention and vain love of singularity' she saw among the clergy, potentially ruinous to the very country itself. 'Such superior and principal officers as you are' were to blame, she went on, for this 'sufferance of sundry varieties and novelties', which constitutes nothing less than 'a great annoyance, trouble and deformity to the rest of the whole body of the realm' and threatens to 'impair, deface, and disturb Christian charity, unity, and concord, being the very bands of our religion'. If Parker was by this time in any doubt about his position in all of this in her eyes, she elaborated even further:

> And although we have now a good while heard to our grief sundry reports hereof, hoping that all cannot be true, but rather mistrusting that the adversaries of truth might of their evil disposition increase the reports of the same: yet we thought, until this present, that by the regard which you, being the primate and metropolitan would have had hereto according to your office, with the assistance of the bishops your brethren in their several dioceses . . . these errors, tending to breed some schism or deformity in the church, should have been stayed and appeased.[56]

The Queen was thus blaming Parker for an impossible and entirely inevitable situation, and demanding he put it right, something even her own explicit royal authority had so far failed to do.

He sought to respond to her as best he could. Further royal declarations would have made his task easier but Elizabeth refused. Parker was thus placed in an impossible position: charged by the Queen in a furious rage to amend an impossibly complex problem, in which people's consciences were at stake, and given by her no further means whatsoever to carry out his instructions. A lesser man would have thrown in the towel. He tried, with Bishop Edmund Grindal, to deal at least with the Diocese of London; although somewhat successful, the two men were nevertheless summoned into the royal presence for a volcanic explosion of impatience and ire. Perhaps, after months of her own growing irritation with the often contrary and frequently self-righteous clergy, the Queen herself needed an outlet through which to channel her anger. She could not have chosen a more unjust target than her Archbishop, 'safe' as he must have seemed. Single-handedly trying to bring the Church of England to order, harried and yet unassisted by the Supreme Governor, he allowed himself an uncharacteristic outburst of exasperation at his isolation, writing to William Cecil:

> The talk, as I am informed, is much increased, and unrestful they be, and I alone they say am in fault. For as for the Queen's Majesty's part, in my expostulation with many of them I signify their disobedience, wherein, because they see the danger, they cease to impute it to her Majesty, for they say, but for my calling on, she is indifferent . . . I only am the stirrer and incenser . . . For my part, I have and do in [good conscience] whatsoever I do. I regard God's honour and then public quiet. I wish obedience to the Queen's Highness and to her laws: the greatest estimation that her Highness can have amongst us. . . . . But for my part, so that my prince may win honour either by standing or relenting, I will be very gladly [the stone of offence[57]].[58]

Parker's 'Advertisements' later in 1566 were the declarations he published of the necessary discipline required of all clergy, and throughout this most testing and trying period of his time as Archbishop, and despite all the Queen's obstinacy and temper, he worked as hard as he could to instil and require the kind of unity in conformity that was so central to any hope of future stability. Nor did he do so without continuing to display his customary compassion and care, even to those who most vociferously opposed him: Thomas Sampson, the Dean of Christ Church, Oxford, was removed from office for refusal to comply, but Parker made sure of his safety, his welfare and that he was well provided for in his loss. Alexander Nowell, the rather radical Dean of St Paul's, made the incredibly brave – or foolish – decision to preach a sermon in front of the Queen, with whom he was already in bad odour because of his public urging of her to marry, against her policy on contested matters. Her outrage was expressed to him, there and then, interrupting his sermon with such venom that Nowell was left 'utterly dismayed'[59] – every preacher's worst nightmare. Although he was probably annoyed at Nowell's behaviour, Parker took him home for dinner, some good wine and a consolatory conversation.

The so-called 'vestiarian' controversy epitomizes the difficulty and the sheer hard work of Parker's time as Archbishop. The weariness in his late letters, to Lord Burghley (as Cecil became in 1571) and his fellow bishops, is palpable, as he found himself endlessly going over the same ground with the 'precisians', seeking to instil in the English Church at the very least a respect for the law as it was established and an understanding of the importance of conformity amid division. When Margaret died in 1570 the job became ever lonelier and less satisfying, and the last five years of Parker's life seem to have been largely unhappy ones both personally and vocationally. But there were highlights: the Queen's visit to Canterbury in 1574, during which she and he spent some time together over the course of several days, was a source of satisfaction for him; his interest in ecclesiastical history never waned and prompted him to collect a remarkable set of ancient manuscripts and books that to this day are preserved at Corpus Christi in the library bearing his name. Further, he set his own hand to a book, the *De Antiquitate Britannicae Ecclesiae*, which sought to outline the independence and authority of his own church, and especially the See of Canterbury, by tracing back to the earliest Church the roots of English Christianity. Designed in part to rebut the claims of Catholic historians like Harpsfield, who died in the same year as Parker and of whose work he was probably aware, the *De Antiquitate* also preserved for future historians some important archival information about the development of some of the characteristic institutions of the Church of England.

In his last surviving letter to Burghley, dictated because of his frailty just a month before his death (an event for which he was by then praying), Parker revealed to the great man his inmost heart in religious matters:

> Does your lordship think that I care either for cap, tippet, surplice, wafer-bread, or any such? But for the laws so established I esteem them, and not more for exercise of contempt against law and authority, which I see will be the end of it, nor for any other respect.[60]

If in some respects these late letters breathe the air of Thomas Cranmer, with their sincere insistence that worldly advancement has meant nothing to him but only the chance to advance the gospel, in this emphasis on conformity over precision in religious doctrine and practice they sound a different note, and one that seems so welcome after decades of turmoil, division, argument, violent disagreement and religious tribalism. It is an outlook that, for all the difficulties and tensions in their relationship, made Parker the perfect Archbishop for the young Elizabeth: the wisdom of knowing you cannot change hearts and minds by force or the threat of it but that you can seek to foster a unity that tolerates diversity of opinion, if only the law will be obeyed. It was a wisdom not always exhibited by his unfortunate successor, Edmund Grindal, who ended his life sequestered and under house arrest for seeking too much his own policy against the wishes of the Queen.

Setting personal happiness aside, Matthew Parker set his hand to the plough and served his monarch and the Church with his characteristic virtues: patient moderation, scholarly insight, pastoral sensitivity and a selfless willingness to absorb the criticism for enforcing another's policy. These were exactly the qualities needed in these difficult and uncertain years: we should not forget the fear felt by many during the 1560s and 1570s that Elizabeth's death would again throw into uncertainty and chaos the Protestant settlement for which they had laboured. Indeed, Parker's last letter to Burghley ends with exactly that prognostication. If he died weary and depressed, his contribution was yet a vital one: it may not be going too far to suggest that, without his approach and his wisdom, Elizabeth's Church could never have been established, and that therefore modern Anglicans owe to this unflashy, humble, quiet scholar far more than they know or often recognize.

7

Governing with Subtlety: Queen Elizabeth I

We begin with two operatic scenes, conceived and composed over a hundred years apart. In the first, the 38-year-old Elizabeth finally meets her cousin and rival, the exiled Mary, Queen of Scots, at Chatsworth. As diplomatic engagements go, it is not a success. Despite Mary's initial humility, falling to her knees and pleading for forgiveness, Elizabeth responds with contempt and describes her desire to see her cousin, whom she has always regarded as haughty, vain and despicable, come to an ignominious end. Mary, provoked by Elizabeth's increasing and overt hostility, finally erupts in one of opera's most famous – and most outrageous – explosions of anger. She calls her royal cousin a 'vil bastarda' (translations are hardly necessary) before cursing the way Anne Boleyn's daughter, an 'unworthy, indecent whore', has dishonoured England's throne for the last 13 years. If she even intended to do so, Mary has not won any friends or influenced anyone in her favour, and her fate is sealed.

The second depicts a much older Queen, at the end of her reign. A rather pathetic figure in her affection for her young courtiers, especially Robert Devereux, the Earl of Essex, and Sir Walter Raleigh, she is nevertheless consumed with jealousy when Lady Essex appears at court in a magnificent dress. Tricking her 'rival' during a costume change, the Queen assumes Lady Essex's dress herself and mocks her favourite's wife cruelly and spitefully, making a fool of herself in the process. Reduced to tears, Lady Essex is crushed and ashamed. Assuming her own clothes again, the Queen switches to regal mode, commissioning Essex as Lord Deputy in Ireland and immediately overcoming the resentment towards her he had just been treacherously expressing. In a following scene, she reflects to William Cecil:

> What fear is, I never knew.
> But as we have authority to rule,
> So we look to be obeyed.

It all makes for great theatre; but these are entirely fictitious scenes. The first opera described, Gaetano Donizetti's *Maria Stuarda*, imagined, in 1834, a meeting between two rival queens that never took place but was the stuff of rich speculation. And it portrayed Elizabeth holding views she never would have countenanced; indeed, her *reluctance* to execute Mary was the biggest obstacle to Cecil's plans for national security in the whole affair. The second, Benjamin Britten's *Gloriana*, first produced in 1953 to mark the coronation of a new young Queen Elizabeth, caused scandal and consternation in following the irreverent biography of Lytton Strachey and thus presenting Elizabeth in a less than flattering light. The imagined scene with Lady Essex is a case in point, a moment in which 'Gloriana' is anything but glorious; rather, flawed, frail, obsessive and envious to the point of humiliation. Nor are her words about fear, quoted above, remotely true: often sleepless, reluctant ever to be left alone, constantly racked with anxiety, the Queen knew fear only too well, both before her accession and long after it. The libretto does, however, more accurately capture her sentiments about her own authority: she expected to be obeyed.

What both these imagined scenes do illustrate, as well as the countless others that have followed them, involving some of the greatest acting talent of any age (Bette Davis, Glenda Jackson, Cate Blanchett), is our endless fascination with an endlessly complex woman. Deprived of many accurate and reliable glimpses into her inmost soul and her most private thoughts, historians try to construct the contents of each based on the evidence we do have. But Elizabeth is difficult to pin down, an enigma wrapped in a puzzle at times. She leaves us guessing: at one moment generous, at another vain and impossibly contrary; here shrewd and insightful, there stubborn and foolish; in one place enduring all manner of personal setback and political frustration with equanimity and poise, in another exploding in volcanic outbursts of ill-temper over apparently trivial nothings. She has left a permanent impression on English history and for ever altered its course and its content, but we may find ourselves, after decades of looking, not much closer to knowing her fully. So it is that for some she is the greatest and most gifted monarch ever to sit on England's throne, and for others she was simply a woman lucky enough to live a long time without misfortune.

Elizabeth Tudor's early life ought to have guaranteed that she would grow up to be a complex personality, even a deeply wounded one. Her childhood was never stable: never knowing her mother, for whom her father had turned the realm and its religion upside down, she was raised in privilege but without much stable affection, except from the ladies-in-waiting who attended the young princess. Her father's own regard for her was warm but she too was subject to the vicissitudes in his attitude, which affected her half sister Mary even more painfully, at one moment acknowledged as his legitimate heir and at another left disowned and unsure of her future. Queen Katherine Parr eventually brought some harmony and a little reconciliation to the family, and her relationship with Elizabeth was consistently fond and engaged, as we have seen. Her husband Thomas Seymour, however, who thought few proprieties applied to him, took unconscionable liberties with the young princess while she stayed with them, and although Elizabeth at 14 seems to have enjoyed both the attention and the flirtatious horseplay, she was too young to be anything other than abused by this arrangement, and left the Seymour household under a cloud, deprived of the company of perhaps the one mother figure she ever knew.

During the turbulent decade during which first her young brother and then her older sister reigned, Elizabeth endured unimaginable stresses and anxieties, which certainly contributed to the lifelong terror we have already noted. Edward, although he shared her Protestant convictions, excluded her from his succession planning quite as much as Mary, whose Catholicism was his primary fear but whose gender was, to his puerile philosophy, also disqualifying. The hypocrisy with which Jane Grey was nevertheless named as his heir was therefore strange: but Elizabeth was not to be its beneficiary. Under Mary, of course, the young princess was famously the victim of all sorts of suspicion, skulduggery and hostility; suspected unjustly of complicity in Wyatt's rebellion of 1554, she spent time in the Tower of London, during which she constantly feared for her life and was subjected to the terrors of interrogation, manipulation and threats. Mary's distrust, and probably dislike of her half-sister, is not entirely unforgivable perhaps, given the circumstances, but she certainly treated Elizabeth with implacable and steely caution, even dread.

Thus when Mary did finally acknowledge that Elizabeth would succeed her upon her imminent death, the 25-year-old who came to the throne in November 1558 was a young woman who had endured all manner of emotional turmoil and personal trauma, and who cannot but have been damaged and wounded by them. Moreover, she assumed the reins of power at a moment of excruciating complexity and political fragility, and relied heavily on the wisdom of her closest adviser, William Cecil, and the extraordinary savvy of her spymaster, Francis Walsingham. Their frequent frustrations with her attitude and her behaviour also amply illustrate the difficulties of working for this brilliant, flawed and determined woman.

It is with religious policy that we are mostly concerned, and here the young woman who became Queen in 1558 seemed oddly, even freakishly, old-fashioned to many of her courtiers and certainly to many of her subjects. She was her father's daughter in this respect, as perhaps in aspects of her temperament. The contours of the religious settlement that she oversaw, as we have seen, seemed incredibly conservative to those who hoped now for a fully fledged English Reformation at last: bishops, clerical vestments, practices at communion that made it seem dangerously similar to the Mass. She legalized clerical marriage again but made very plain her own strong distaste for it, as Margaret Parker discovered. She really would have preferred that her priests kept their wives hidden than be forced to acknowledge the reality of her own legislation. Most scandalous of all, and the greatest source of annoyance and disbelieving frustration for the more ardent reformers, was her crucifix, kept stubbornly on the altar of the Chapel Royal. Visiting preachers railed against it; pamphleteers excoriated it as a Catholic hangover, a papist relic, a superstitious canker at the heart of the nation's life; braver bishops urged her to remove it. All was in vain. Nor was such advice ever gratefully received. The Queen knew what she liked.

Those who longed for further reform, of course, assumed that the caution of the 1558–9 Settlement was merely a stopgap. Perhaps, in time, even the crucifix would disappear, as bishoprics gave way to presbyteries and copes and surplices to Geneva gowns. Once Catholicism was banished from the realm again, and the young Queen's assurance and confidence grew, a full and thoroughgoing Reformation would emerge and be implemented – they hoped. But despite her youth, Elizabeth was never one for the latest trend or the newest continental fad. She saw the Settlement as the last word, not only the first. And she refused, against all effort to persuade her otherwise, to alter one jot or tittle of any of it. Even Matthew Parker's infamous 'Advertisements' were the result of her iron-willed determination to alter nothing, even in the smallest detail, of what had been established in those early weeks of her reign. She had taken as her motto, *Semper Eadem*: always the same. She followed it, even to a fault. The moderation of her Church of England, the 'middle way' of Anglicanism, this halfway house between Lutheranism and Reformed Christianity, owes much of its DNA to an intransigent monarch who seemed to many of her subjects impossibly out of date, even in 1559.

For all that, there was great genius in this too, and genius that the times so desperately needed. Francis Bacon described how the Queen said that she made it a virtue not to 'make windows on to men's souls': after decades of uncertainty, continual change and even religious persecution, a moderately Protestant Church to which one merely had openly to conform and in which no inquisitions would be held was a remarkable and wonderful thing. Thus even the 'Church Papists' – Catholics who retained their loyalties to Rome even while they accepted Elizabeth's legitimacy – could simply attend the parish services on Sunday, and carry on believing in their hearts whatever they wished, as long as they made no disturbances to the commonwealth because of them. Thus too the 'precisians', as long as they did the same, were welcome to covet whatever kind of future evolution they wanted in the Church's life, as well as look down on its 'medieval' hangovers with self-righteous disdain and disapproval. Elizabeth and her ministers finally laid the foundations for a national Church broad enough to encompass a variety of opinions and generous enough not to scratch too deeply beneath the surface of anyone's conformity. If this seems quite illiberal to us, it was in fact, for its day, the wisest possible course and smacks much more of modern notions of freedom of conscience than anything much seen up to this point in Tudor England – or, for that matter, in continental Europe, in which Calvin's Geneva was no more tolerant of difference and disagreement than had been the terrifying prophets of Zwickau in the 1520s.

Human nature being what it is, however, conformity to a Settlement that did not exactly reflect their sense of the True Church was never going to satisfy many, on whichever side of the Reformation debates they dwelt. Whatever the strangeness and eclecticism of her own religious preferences, Elizabeth felt that endless innovation in ecclesial matters was only going to make matters worse. There was never any possibility of moving closer to Rome, or of doing anything to deny her own legitimacy or her governorship of the Church of England. Nor, however, was she ever persuaded by the appeals of men like Thomas Cartwright, the

Lady Margaret Professor of Divinity in Cambridge, or Lawrence Humphrey, the President of Magdalen College, Oxford, who publicly and persistently decried England's partial Reformation and her fatal compromise with idolatry and popery. As time passed without further change, as even the more radical bishops became champions of Elizabeth's Church, and as moderation entrenched itself as the watchword, the possibility of further change receded into the far distance. Added to that, as the Settlement under the steady leadership of Parker and his allies bedded in and became more and more familiar in parishes across the land, events were about to strengthen the Queen's hand and redouble her tenacity.

In February 1570, Pope Pius V issued a bull, *Regnans in Excelsis*, whose consequences for English Catholics then and for centuries to come were cataclysmic. Elizabeth, the Pope insisted, was a 'pretended Queen'; he savaged her faithlessness in reversing the advances made back towards Catholicism under Mary, and her heretical actions in foisting on the English her own ecclesiastical policies and practices. Then came the main thrust:

And moreover we declare her to be deprived of her pretended title to the aforesaid crown and of all lordship, dignity and privilege whatsoever;

And also declare the nobles, subjects and people of the said realm and all others who have in any way sworn oaths to her, to be forever absolved from such an oath and from any duty arising from lordship, fealty and obedience; and we do, by authority of these presents, so absolve them and so deprive the same Elizabeth of her pretended title to the crown and all other the above said matters. We charge and command all and singular the nobles, subjects, peoples and others afore said that they do not dare obey her orders, mandates and laws. Those who shall act to the contrary we include in the like sentence of excommunication.[61]

For English Catholics, a mere expectation of open conformity no longer seemed like a safe policy. All of them were now under suspicion: adherence to the Pope's orders by any of them would have constituted treason. Pius' invitation to the English to contemplate open rebellion against, and the overthrow of, their monarch could not be ignored – by either side.

The climate this all created in the 1570s and beyond was febrile and often intensely fraught. Elizabeth, too, despite her constant and habitual anxiety amid the stress of rule and the danger of assassination, was coming into her own as she progressed into middle age and became more assured and instinctive about the practice of government. Her ministers did not always find her growing self-confidence helpful. In particular, and in contrast to the kind of scenario envisaged by Donizetti's librettist Giuseppe Bardari (influenced by Schiller) in 1834, she increasingly resisted their counsel concerning the woman who, more than any other individual, embodied and represented the threat to her reign from the Catholic powers of Europe: her cousin Mary, the overthrown Queen of Scotland and political asylum seeker, whom Elizabeth had, in 1568, taken in. As long as Mary was alive, she would always attract the hopes of those who longed for Elizabeth's overthrow – hopes that Mary foolishly courted and entertained, unfailingly attracted by the lustre of power. Once again, however, Elizabeth refused to adjust her old-fashioned principles, even in an age of conspiracy and danger. The result was that even as her life and reign were threatened, she could not, would not, take the step that Cecil thought indispensable, and kill a fellow Queen, especially one who shared her blood.

Walsingham's discovery of the Babington plot in 1586, the latest in a series of moves to kill Elizabeth and replace her with Mary, finally brought the Scottish Queen down. Careless and incautious in her dealings with the plotters, and allured by the prospect of seizing the English throne, Mary's correspondence betrayed her, and her lack of circumspection was no match for Walsingham's methods. He and Cecil – who had been created

Baron Burghley in 1571 – insisted that only Mary's execution could ever subdue the incessant plotting and manoeuvring surrounding her and threatening Elizabeth, but she in her turn was fiercely resistant to the idea of killing her cousin. Monarchs, in her view, whatever their religion, were God's own anointed and could not be so casually disposed of. It could not be right, she firmly believed, to seek to avoid her own murder by committing the crime of regicide against a sister queen. And so Elizabeth avoided, dodged and resisted Burghley's efforts to seal Mary's fate. Finally she was persuaded that Mary's death was the only thing that could bring about some safety and stability. When her efforts to inveigle Mary's custodian into smothering her unsurprisingly failed, she was eventually prevailed upon to sign a death warrant. The hapless William Davison, however, the courtier to whom she entrusted it, was given clear instructions that he was not to relinquish the document until given permission, instructions that Burghley was able to ignore. Mary died at Fotheringhay early in 1587. A genuinely horrified Elizabeth, furious to have been tricked, imprisoned Davison and banished Burghley from her presence, causing a breach in their relationship that barely healed in the remaining decade of his life.

Frustrating as Elizabeth's behaviour and shifting attitudes to the problem of Mary must have been for Burghley and her Council, attempting to deal with the real dangers to the realm and the realpolitik of the age, there was a consistency to them. She loathed war and for the most part resisted violence, until and unless there was a direct and imminent danger to her own safety. Her ministers had grown used to her deep resistance to committing English forces to support continental allies – in the Netherlands, for instance, or against the growing Spanish threat. When those around her tried to force her hand or even took matters into their own, as did Robert Dudley in the Netherlands in 1586, accepting the title of Governor General against her explicit desire, the consequences for their position and standing could be terrible. The predatory incursions of her ambitious young favourites into the territory of English enemies, as at Cadiz, filled her with dread and dismay. She had none of her father's passion for war, or for the expansion of the borders of the realm by military force. Elizabeth longed only for peace, for a settled period of consolidation.

Again, as with religious policy, the Queen sometimes pursued this virtual pacifism even when it left her and the realm even more exposed. Burghley regularly had to beg her to be tougher in shoring up against foreign threats and in deploying the armed forces in English interests. When the Spanish did eventually bring the fight to the English Channel in 1588, Elizabeth's fleet was ready to meet the mighty Armada only really because of the efforts of her commanders, against her own apparent intransigence. Her famous appearance at Tilbury, the stuff of legend, was undertaken quite against her own instincts, at the instigation of Dudley, and at a point at which the Spanish were in fact already overcome. Very soon afterwards, too, the goodwill she had engendered on the occasion was lost, as she failed to make good on her promises to reward the conscripts for their loyalty and service. The Queen simply disliked war and all its surrounding infrastructure. It was a deep aversion to violence that she also applied to the murder of anointed monarchs, even if they were implicated in treason against her.

Against the Roman Catholic threat more broadly, however, Elizabeth over time became less averse to the use of violence. If the papal declaration of 1570 left many Catholics in a fearfully vulnerable position, it also opened the door to a new style of missionary activity, both among the English 'recusants' – Catholics who could not in all conscience recognize the ecclesiastical supremacy of the Queen or the validity of her Church – and beyond. The renewal of Catholicism that was formerly known as the 'Counter-Reformation'[62] was underway, evident both in the confident doctrinal assertions of the Council of Trent and in the flowering of new religious orders whose primary purpose and aim was to re-instil Catholic spirituality and a connectedness to Rome all across those parts of Europe that had embraced

Protestantism. Foremost among these was the Society of Jesus, founded in 1540 by the dynamic and visionary Ignatius Loyola for the re-evangelization of the Holy Land, but actually finding its mission all across Protestant Europe, its focus less on Muslim conversion than on winning back the Evangelicals. Jesuits, as the members of this vigorous order became known, began to be trained in seminaries on the continent and sent as missionary priests to the isolated and vilified Catholic community in England. For Elizabeth, they represented a dire threat to the stability of her Settlement and thus of the realm.

It is a mark of the extent to which English prejudice against Roman Catholicism took root in and after this period that the ferocity with which these missionaries and their flock were treated causes so little shock or disgust. While John Foxe was able to fix Mary Tudor for ever in the popular imagination as 'Bloody Mary', cruel and intent on all manner of brutality against Protestants, it is rarely remembered that over 200 Catholics were killed in late Elizabethan England, and that the methods used to interrogate, confine and then execute them far surpassed anything devised even in Marian times. Priests like Robert Southwell, hung in irons by his wrists until his blood vessels burst, then taken down and strung up again as soon as he had sufficiently recovered, might have preferred the rack. Certainly, the fate of traitors, as these men were deemed to be, was far more ghastly even than to be burned alive – especially those who were dismembered while still fully conscious, like William Parry in 1585. Parry was implicated in a plot to assassinate the Queen; but men like Southwell maintained the legitimacy and authority of her rule, and claimed only to be providing the sacraments to isolated Catholics. The dearth of any evidence against him did not prevent his torture, his imprisonment in the most disgusting and sordid surroundings, including the infamous 'Limbo' in the Tower, and his execution in 1595, which came as a blessed relief after years of such treatment.

Over time, of course, the mere fact of being Catholic was enough to convict men and women of treason, such was the effect of the papal proclamation of 1570 and such the clear and present danger of that small minority of the Catholic community who did see Elizabeth's removal as the only possible way to the reintroduction of 'true' religion again. Those whose aims were more pastoral and priestly, however, demonstrated extraordinary courage and a passionate intensity of faithful action in seeking to carry out their mission. Edmund Campion, who had come over in the first wave of activity in the 1580s, put it rather touchingly and memorably in his *Ten Reasons* of 1581, addressed to the Privy Council but intended for wide circulation. Its readers could resent and dispute the assertion of Catholic truth it contained, but they could not ignore the document's transparent sincerity and bravery:

> I doubt not but you her Highness' Council being, of such wisdom and discreet in cases most important, when you shall have heard these questions of religion opened faithfully, which many times by our adversaries are huddled up and confounded, will see upon what substantial grounds our Catholic Faith is builded, how feeble that side is which by sway of the time prevaileth against us, and so at last for your own souls, and for many thousand souls that depend upon your government, will discountenance error when it is bewrayed, and hearken to those who would spend the best blood in their bodies for your salvation. Many innocent hands are lifted up to heaven for you daily by those English students, whose posterity shall never die, which beyond seas gathering virtue and sufficient knowledge for the purpose, are determined never to give you over, but either to win you heaven, or to die upon your pikes. And touching our Society be it known to you that we have made a league – all the Jesuits in the world, whose succession and multitude must overreach all the practices of England – cheerfully to carry the cross you shall lay upon us, and never to despair your recovery, while we have a man left to enjoy your Tyburn, or to be racked with your torments, or consumed with

your prisons. The expense is reckoned, the enterprise is begun; it is of God, it cannot be withstood. So the faith was planted: so it must be restored.

Equally moving was the way Campion echoed and reflected the spirit of saints like Thomas More in his ardent love for his land and its people, and in his hope of better, less contentious days, in the next life if not in this:

> If these my offers be refused, and my endeavours can take no place, and I, having run thousands of miles to do you good, shall be rewarded with rigour, I have no more to say but to recommend your case and mine to Almighty God, the Searcher of Hearts, who send us His grace, and set us at accord before the day of payment, to the end we may at last be friends in heaven, when all injuries shall be forgotten.[63]

Yet Elizabeth set her face implacably against Campion and his kind, in this area uniquely determined that violent repression should stamp out a foreign threat and what she saw as a hostile religious force. She encouraged the appalling methods and the horrifying cruelty of her torturer Richard Topcliffe; she insisted on the severest penalties for those infiltrating the kingdom with their Roman Catholic subversion; she personally approved of a ferocious policy of zero tolerance. Doubtless many factors were at work – her own sleepless anxiety about her safety; her stubborn determination that her religious settlement should last; her genuine convictions about royal supremacy; her outrage at any threat to the stability of the realm or any resistance of her command; and the clear and urgent advice of her ministers – but Elizabeth's anti-Catholic policies were fearful indeed.

She was equally implacable – if not quite so violent in the expression of her outrage – against those on the other end of the religious spectrum. The Puritans, as they became known, never ceased to make known their deep disappointment and intense grief at England's pathetic and inadequate Reformation. Over time they developed their own subculture, not unlike that of the Roman Catholics except possessing the freedom to be more overt and thus to challenge the authorities openly. In cracking down on Puritan resistance, too, the Queen had less support from many of her ministers than against the Catholics. Never much of a Protestant when it came to preaching, she preferred a more predictable liturgy, partly fed up herself at the use of the pulpit as a vehicle from which to criticize her own policies. Thus arose a great and calamitous dispute with Archbishop Edmund Grindal, Parker's successor at Canterbury. It concerned the practice of 'prophesyings', local Bible studies, open to laity and ordained clergy, which Evangelicals like the Archbishop thought helpful places for the inculcation of scriptural knowledge and the encouragement of godly discourse. The Queen thought them dangerous and ill-disciplined. When Grindal flatly refused to enforce her ban on them, he was sequestered from office and spent several years effectively under house arrest. Once again, those who hoped that the religious settlement of the late 1550s was merely a staging post were left in no doubt of her intentions.

Grindal's own successor, John Whitgift, was chosen because he more closely mirrored Elizabeth's hostility towards Puritanism and shared her desire to curb its public defiance. He came to the job after a distinguished academic career at Cambridge, during the course of which he had already deprived the Presbyterian Thomas Cartwright of his professorial chair, and after a decade as Bishop of Worcester, where his anti-Puritan zeal had also been put into practice against diocesan clergy. After a period of time in exile, Cartwright returned to England in the 1580s and proceeded to be no less controversial than he had been in Cambridge in his advocacy of what he believed to be clear New Testament principles. These included a fully Reformed Church in England that dispensed with bishops, kneeling to receive communion, and all other Roman Catholic hangovers. In resisting him and his associates, Elizabeth and Whitgift did not enjoy the full support of key members of her Council: Burghley, for one, harboured sympathies with many Puritan demands, which meant that, behind the scenes at least, he worked to moderate the punishment of their proponents.

The Elizabethan Puritan movement, rather similarly to the Roman Catholic community, had its conformists and its more radical fringe. Among the former were men like William Perkins, a Cambridge don whose writings and advocacy exercised huge influence among the 'precisians', even while he himself insisted on outward obedience to the law. Perkins was a key conduit for Calvinist theology into England, a stalwart champion of 'double' predestination on the grounds that it was of inestimable comfort to know that one's destiny was safe in God's hands and not dependent on one's own efforts. A defender of those prosecuted for their views, his own conformity generally ensured his safety. Irritating though he was to them, his was the kind of dissent with which the regime found it easiest to deal. More troubling was the emerging satirical literature against the Elizabethan Church: its anonymity, wide circulation and biting mockery of the establishment proved very effective. Beginning in 1588, a series of tracts written by one 'Martin Marprelate' was published, excoriating the ecclesiastical authorities with savage wit, scurrilous rumour, lewd invective and even a little theological argument. The bishops, 'proud, popish, presumptuous, profane, paltry, pestilent and pernicious prelates', as the tracts described them, were the butt of the humour (although they found little in them to laugh at). Although the publisher was eventually arrested and prosecuted, 'Martin Marprelate' was never identified. The Queen, like her nineteenth-century descendant, was not amused. Her Church's divisions and contentions grew ever deeper, laid bare in public satire late into her reign.

All of which, perhaps, does little more than illustrate the opening claim of this chapter: that Queen Elizabeth I was immensely complex. The soul on to which it would be most difficult to gain a window is her own. While her ministers and counsellors went home to hearth, spouse and children, she, partly by choice and partly by necessity, was denied such comforts and such confidants. Hers was a supremely lonely existence, a solemn and enormous responsibility that she bore for 45 years. In that light, and with knowledge of her difficult and dangerous youth, it becomes possible to admire her virtues a little more and condemn her foibles and failures a little less. Her folly in her choice of favourites, supremely in her patronage of the rash and reckless Robert Devereux in her final years, surely echoed her own sense of the crushing solitude of her position and her desire for human connection and warmth, perhaps even intimacy, of a rather chaste kind. Her insistence on the obedience of her subjects was nothing too unusual for the day, especially in one whose views were as nostalgic as hers: Elizabeth was the granddaughter of Henry VII and the daughter of Henry VIII in adopting this attitude, more than the cousin of King James VI of Scotland, who looked for much clearer and more honest counsel from his advisers and was soon to be a breath of fresh air in Elizabeth's old court.

Semper Eadem: always one and the same. Her motto was the watchword of her reign. If to some her adoption of this rule of life signified intransigence, a stubborn refusal to move with the times or adjust to the prevailing winds, to many others it was a remarkable sign of an extraordinary faithfulness. This faithfulness, of course, ultimately came to be seen as embodied and symbolized in her virginity. As her reign moved towards its fortieth year, 'Gloriana', the Virgin Queen, who had married her realm and denied herself personal happiness in order to promote its stability and peace, became a figure of mythic proportions. Something of that iconic status has remained. And yet beneath it we can still glimpse the young woman, intellectually brilliant, fiery in temper and generous in friendship, terrified of the weight of her duty and yet the most equipped of all the Tudors to discharge it, who first began her public service aged just 25.

We can glimpse her faith, too, as the bedrock of that faithfulness. Elizabeth's religious policy was in some sense a matter of law, as Matthew Parker conceded on his deathbed. Conformity to it was an expression of loyalty to her, but it made no fundamentalist claims of inerrancy: you submitted to the Church of England as a sign of your love for the Queen. But Elizabeth's own religion was a different matter. Her tastes and preferences were eccentric and curious, perhaps, but they were built around a devotion and a piety that long years of often lonely rule only fostered. A prayer book written by her around 1580, somewhat in the style of her stepmother Katherine Parr, gives us one of those glimpses of her own deep reliance on her faith. Although composed in a necessarily formal way, the final prayer, in its heartfelt phrases, its frequent biblical allusion and its tender vulnerability, surely reflects the deepest desires of the heart of this frustrating, flawed, fascinating and ultimately admirable and attractive woman:

> O Lord God, Father everlasting, which reignest over the kingdoms of men and givest them at Thy pleasure, which of Thy great mercy hast chosen me Thy servant and handmaid to feed Thy people and Thine inheritance; so teach me, I humbly beseech Thee, Thy Word and so strengthen me with Thy grace that I may feed Thy people with a faithful and a true heart, and rule them prudently with power. O Lord, Thou hast set me on high; my flesh is frail and weak. If I therefore at any time forget Thee, touch my heart, O Lord, that I may again remember Thee. If I swell against Thee, pluck me down in my own conceit, that Thou mayest raise me in Thy sight. Grant me, O Lord, a listening ear to hear Thee and a hungry soul to long after Thy Word. Endue me with Thy heavenly Spirit. Give me Thy Spirit of wisdom that I may understand Thee. Give me Thy Spirit of truth, that I may know Thee, Thy feeling Spirit that I may fear Thee, Thy Spirit of grace that I may love Thee, Thy Spirit of zeal that I may hunger and thirst after Thee, Thy persevering Spirit that I may live and dwell and reign with Thee.

I acknowledge, O my King, without Thee my throne is unstable, my seat unsure, my kingdom tottering, my life uncertain. I see all things in this life subject to mutability, nothing to continue still at one stay; but fear and trembling, hunger and thirst, cold and heat, weakness and faintness, sorrow and sickness, doth evermore oppress mankind. I hear how ofttimes untimely death doth carry away the mightiest and greatest personages. I have learned out of Thy holy Word that horrible judgement is nigh unto them which walk not after Thy will, and the mighty, swerving from Thy law, shall be mightily tormented. Therefore sith all things in this world, both heaven and earth, shall pass and perish and Thy Word alone endureth forever, engraft, O most gracious Lord Christ, this Thy Word of grace and life so in my heart that from henceforth I neither follow after feigned comforts in worldly power, neither distract my mind to transitory pleasures, nor occupy my thoughts in vain delights, but that carefully seeking Thee where Thou showest Thyself in Thy Word, I may surely find Thee to my comfort and everlastingly enjoy Thee to my salvation.

Create therefore in me, O Lord, a new heart and so renew my spirit within me that Thy law may be my study, Thy truth my delight, Thy Church my care, Thy people my crown, Thy righteousness my pleasure, Thy service my government, Thy fear my honour, Thy grace my strength, Thy favour my life, Thy Gospel my kingdom, and Thy salvation my bliss and my glory. So shall this my kingdom through Thee be established with peace; so shall Thy Church be edified with power; so shall Thy Gospel be published with zeal; so shall my reign be continued with prosperity; so shall my life be prolonged with happiness; and so shall myself at Thy good pleasure be translated into immortality. Which, O merciful Father, grant for the merit of Thy Son Jesus Christ, to whom with the Holy Ghost be rendered all praise and glory forever. Amen.[64]

8

The Piety of Prayer and the Fluency of Speech: Lancelot Andrewes

To have sat in a pew beneath the pulpit of Lancelot Andrewes, and to have heard him preach, must have been one of the most transporting experiences of the late sixteenth and early seventeenth centuries. Today, even reading his impeccable, stirring, creative, mercurial prose is a wonder, inviting the reader, as once he invited his listeners, to explore scriptural texts and doctrinal formulations in new and undreamed-of ways. Andrewes' wordplay is sparkling; he wrests from a single drop of language, even a single word, an ocean of meaning, each insight more remarkable than the last, every clause essential, with not a sentence wasted. Although in his way, Lancelot Andrewes made quite as important a contribution to emerging Anglican thought as some of his more famous contemporaries, he is the fountainhead of the Church of England's preaching tradition, as well as of much of its devotional practice.

Small wonder, then, that he has been claimed by subsequent generations of Anglicans as a key influence in their own development and understanding. Unsurprisingly too, the claims made for his influence have not always been altogether accurate. In 1927 the American poet T. S. Eliot, by then living in London, announced his conversion to Anglicanism from the Unitarianism of his youth and upbringing. Not only that, but he converted to a particular expression of the Church of England's broad tradition, the Anglo-Catholic wing, heavily influenced by the Oxford Movement of the previous century and by its claims to and insistence on the Church's faithful connections to Roman

Catholic tradition and thought. Later that year he adopted British citizenship and renounced his US inheritance. The following year his book, *For Lancelot Andrewes: Essays on Style and Order*, further claimed that his conversion, and his basic vision of the Church to which he had attached himself, was hugely indebted to what he had discovered, reading the work of this seventeenth-century divine.

Eliot was not the first to accord Andrewes such a critical role in identifying and then shaping the essential character of the Church of England and its doctrine and practice. The 'Tractarians' of the Oxford Movement themselves had seen in his writings some of the resources they sought in their efforts to shift their Church back towards what they understood to be its authentic centre of gravity. Before them, however, some of Andrewes' key understandings of Christian theology, some of the elements of his own espousal of authentic Christianity that resonated throughout his sermons, prayers and writings, had been influential in some rather different figures. His insistence on the practice of personal piety, his fondness for the Eastern Christian notion of 'theosis' (of which more soon) and his rigorous application of biblical texts to contemporary issues have been claimed as central and hugely significant for John and Charles Wesley, whose Evangelical revivalism of the eighteenth century seemed far removed from the later concerns of Newman, Keble and Pusey. They, and many leading Anglicans of the decades preceding them, saw his methods as distinctively Anglican, laying the groundwork for a whole way of approaching the faith. In the twentieth century, one of Andrewes' main admirers and champions was a Russian Orthodox scholar, Nicolas Lossky.

Before we test the validity of these competing and striking claims, we should meet the man in his own time. With Andrewes, we are moving into a new generation. Born in 1555, his formative memories were all of the Elizabethan age. He knew nothing at first hand of the struggles, vicissitudes and competing claims of the earlier Tudors' reigns. Raised and formed in the stable environment of the Church of England as established and settled in 1559, Andrewes' concerns were thus very different from those of Cranmer or Parker. He and his generation were in some ways freer to seek to define the character and the mission of their Church and to place it in its mature form against the Church in every place and time. They came to do so with evident pride in it, and with confidence in the Church of England's distinctive contribution to the Church Universal.

Those like Eliot who have sought to claim Lancelot Andrewes as a sort of nineteenth-century High Churchman, out of his time and context, have often forgotten that his own formation, in Elizabethan Cambridge, was quite distinctively Puritan. Educated under the shadow of non-conformists like Thomas Cartwright, and in the rather radical atmosphere of Pembroke Hall, Andrewes' early career reflects the emphases of his environment. In fact the inculcation of Puritan values and approaches in his younger life goes back even further: born into the home of a former mariner and trader, in Barking, Lancelot was almost certainly raised an Evangelical by his father Thomas. It is likely that the love of and saturation in Scripture that characterizes his sermons owes everything to this early influence, as well as to both the kind of curriculum and the extra-curricular activities that Pembroke, with its regular 'prophesyings', would have offered.

In any case, Andrewes was a brilliant scholar. A fellow of Pembroke by 1578, just seven years after arriving as an undergraduate, he was made Master in 1589, aged 34. In any period he would have stood out as one of the great intellects of the age: a voracious linguist, he is said to have mastered 15 languages, using vacations back in London, and his father's global connections, to acquire a new one like a compulsive collector. Steeped particularly in classical languages, he immersed himself absolutely in the writings of the Church 'Fathers', the key theologians of the first five centuries of the Church, both Eastern and Western, whom he took to be critical in the establishing of any claim, by any Church, to possess authority and authenticity. So extraordinarily comprehensive was his mastery of these 'patristic' authors that he quoted from them freely and from memory, his own pattern of thought indissolubly shaped and formed by theirs. As one of his more recent commentators put it, Lancelot Andrewes 'seems to think *with* the Fathers rather than merely to furnish extracts out of their writings'.[65] Clearly, this dazzling polymath, if he so chose, had a glittering career ahead.

Andrewes was also deeply affected by the wider events of these formative years. The Spanish Armada attacked English shores in 1588, just as he was beginning to be noticed by and make friendships with those close to power. He became the Chaplain to the Earl of Huntingdon, who as President of the Council of the North was responsible for enforcing government policy against some strongly Catholic communities. His prime connection to the Queen at this time was the intelligence chief Sir Francis Walsingham, whose patronage was vital to his subsequent promotion and preferment. So just when the Roman Catholic threat to England's settled polity was at its greatest, Lancelot Andrewes was being introduced to the circles of power and the life of the royal court, which were later to play such a large part in his career. The 'foreign' Catholic threat – and its terrifying manifestation in a well-armed fleet in the English Channel – was no trifling or romantic thing to someone coming to the height of their powers at this moment. Andrewes' later admirers therefore miss something of his own stamp in ignoring the very Protestant feelings he had towards Roman Catholicism.

Lancelot Andrewes could have risen higher and faster had he chosen. Although he turned down early offers of episcopal office under Elizabeth, he was still clearly a talent on the rise. He became Vicar of St Giles, Cripplegate, in the City of London, and prebend at both St Paul's and Southwell. This kind of 'plurality', or holding of multiple church appointments (and thus incomes), was nothing unusual at the time, and clearly further marked him out as one to watch. Nor in fact did he treat these appointments as purely honorary, choosing to spend a good deal of time at St Paul's in particular, where his distinctive attitudes were becoming more clear, as in his unusual practice of hearing confession. His reading of those early Church writings had convinced him that this was something whose wisdom and usefulness was well attested and not merely a Roman Catholic innovation.

These kinds of appointments, the world in which he now moved and above all his continued, disciplined, reading of early Christian thought were shaping Andrewes's mature theology. By the end of Elizabeth's reign he was drawn into the controversy surrounding the Marprelate Tracts, and the hunt for their authors, as well as other efforts to crack down on separatism and extreme Calvinism in the Church of England. The crowning achievement in terms of his career advancement at this time was to be made Dean of Westminster in 1600. He was thus one of Archbishop Whiftgift's key allies in the ongoing struggle for conformity to Elizabeth's Settlement as her life came to an end and the new century dawned. As James VI of Scotland, finally and gratefully named by the Queen as her heir, rode south to take up his new, soon to be united kingdoms, Lancelot Andrewes prepared to oversee the arrangements for the King's coronation.

The relationship between him and the new King turned into a vital one. James' efforts to continue the kind of conciliation and moves towards conformity of his predecessor, as well as his vision for the eccentric, episcopal Church of which he now found himself Supreme Governor, needed exactly the learning, wisdom and flair of men like Lancelot Andrewes. He was therefore an obvious invitee to the Hampton Court Conference of 1604, called in an attempt to forge some mediation between the often bitter ongoing disputes of the English Church. The main fruit of that meeting was the agreement to produce a new translation of the English Bible, designed in large part to satisfy the Puritans' insistent demands for such an edition, fit for a new century and new circumstances. The polyglot Andrewes was again the obvious candidate to play a leading role, and so he did, not only heading up the group that translated the first section of the Hebrew Scriptures (Genesis to

2 Kings) but also playing a directing part in the bringing together of the whole – a monumental achievement, which was published in 1611. In a characteristically unostentatious way, the man in the editorial background thus made a great impact on English Christianity and identity for centuries to come.

The changes King James made to diocesan governance, reducing royal interference particularly in financial matters, allowed Andrewes to entertain offers of episcopal promotion, having been unable to do so under Elizabeth's more intrusive approach. In 1605 he accepted the See of Chichester, resigning all his other preferments and appointments to undertake a task he viewed as sacred. In the same year he was appointed Court Preacher, the role in which he made the greatest impact, preaching before the monarch at Christmas, Easter, Whitsun and other ceremonial occasions annually. This was a pivotal year in one other crucial respect: just days after accepting Chichester, the new bishop was among those gathered in Parliament on the fifth of November, conscious that, but for the vigilance of the security forces he, along with King and parliamentary personnel, would have been savagely murdered. The Gunpowder Plot, like the Armada, was a searing memory in the English imagination; one of Andrewes' yearly duties as Court Preacher would henceforth be to commemorate the salvation the day commemorated. He did so enthusiastically, no doubt for ever mindful himself of the narrowness of his own escape, let alone the national anarchy Guy Fawkes and his associates had intended to bring about.

Despite the onerous nature of his other commitments and appointments, Andrewes was a diligent diocesan bishop, organizing for careful visitations in the parishes to ensure the orderliness of worship and the proper provision of liturgy and pastoral care, as well as testing the probity of clergy. This, and the high profile he enjoyed in his other appointments, brought continued promotion, to larger and richer dioceses: Ely, in 1609, and finally Winchester in 1618. In all these places he was known for his cultivation of a prayerful, scholarly life, continuing to set aside mornings and evenings for his own study and devotion, and assiduous in the remaining hours of the day in his duties and responsibilities as bishop.

Although they disagreed in some matters of theology, Lancelot Andrewes and King James were close allies in the governing of the Church and realm. Indeed, Andrewes' own beliefs about kingship were rather 'high', to the extent that sometimes his mature judgement might have been impaired by his absolute commitment to the divine rights of anointed kings and queens. The most notorious example of this occurred in 1613 when he was drafted to give judgement in the salacious and very complex matter of the divorce of the Earl of Essex. This Earl was the son of Elizabeth's favourite Robert Devereux, who had ultimately been executed for treacherous actions against the Queen arising from a sustained fit of jealous pique. The Earl's Countess, Frances Howard, wanted to be free of their marriage in order, quite scandalously, to pursue a new relationship with Robert Carr, the Viscount Rochester. Rochester was a close friend of King James, who made his own preference for the divorce to be swiftly granted very clear and rather public. Andrewes, appointed to the divorce hearing, was not normally the kind of man to bend to such overt infidelity and lustful intent. Doubtless influenced by the King, he did exactly that. During the course of the hearings, however, all manner of details emerged on both sides concerning matters of a highly intimate nature in the noble marriage. No one emerged without embarrassment or taint, least of all the supposedly saintly Bishop of Ely, who turned out to be just as biddable as everyone else, at least where kings' orders were involved.

More understandably, and much less controversially, Andrewes was also asked by the King's ministers to turn his formidable gifts to polemical work against Rome. Although this kind of genre was not instinctive for him, he set his shoulder to the wheel and took on the leading Catholic spokesman, Cardinal Robert Bellarmine. Bellarmine had begun to write against the English government in the wake of the Gunpowder Plot, and in particular had sought to undermine the English monarch's authority to command the obedience of his or her subjects. Shaped by his personal outrage, having witnessed the consequences of the dangers of popes ordering subjects to disobey their monarchs and their nation's laws, as well as by his vast learning, Andrewes produced two works of careful and subsequently influential ecclesiology. Doing so gave him a chance to make a contribution, too, to the wider effort to define the Church of England and assert its own continuity with the marks of the True Church revealed in Scripture and history. Thus he resisted not only the claims of Roman Catholics, that 'catholicity', or membership of the authentic Church comes as a result of being subject to papal supremacy and control, but also those of the more extreme Calvinists. They taught that only God knew – only God could know – the 'invisible' Church, made up of the elect, and that therefore all earthly structures were of secondary importance compared to this kind of hidden- but real -belonging. Deploying a devastating range of sources, theologians, authorities and examples, Andrewes portrayed the Church of England's catholicity, proven and demonstrated through its continuity with earliest Christianity, and exemplified in its system of episcopacy, which he understood to be one sign of it. In doing so, he undermined the claims of both Catholics and Calvinists in one fell stroke.

Such a survey of Lancelot Andrewes' career, though, impressive and consequential as it was, doesn't come close to doing justice to his contribution. This is because it is as a preacher and a wordsmith he is best known, and so we cannot really gain a proper sense of his brilliance as an orator – or indeed the beauty of his theology – without encountering some examples of his work. Those set-piece court sermons, several times a year, as well as the less publicized occasions, in St Giles or Westminster or one of his dioceses, solidified his reputation as one of the greatest preachers ever to take up a pulpit in the Church of England. The craft of the delivery matched the dazzling insight of his biblical interpretation and theological reflection, mirroring not only his rhetorical skill but also his saturation in the finest minds of Christian antiquity. Therefore taking just the tiniest cross section of his output, let us sample his genius and understand better his characteristic emphases.

It's appropriate that Christmas and Easter were two of the annual occasions requiring his gifts, as the doctrines of incarnation (God taking flesh in Jesus Christ) and resurrection (Jesus' rising from death and then ascending to heaven) were absolutely central to Andrewes' own understanding of the core Christian message and appeal to humanity. He was viscerally drawn to the widespread teaching of the early Church sometimes called 'interchange': that, in Christ, God was pouring Godself into humanity so that humanity, in experiencing the fullness of God's life in a human life, might in turn be restored to the whole stature of God's image within us. Irenaeus, the second-century Bishop of Lyons, had summarized it most vividly in asserting that 'God became what we are in order to make us what God is'; he later won widespread agreement among the writers with whom Andrewes spent his time, among them some of the greatest names in Christian theology: Athanasius, Augustine and the two Gregorys, of Nyssa and Nazianzus. It was a doctrine Andrewes sought to expound, in his turn, in language fit for seventeenth-century England, believing it to be the central transformative claim of the Christian faith and the only possible reason for hope of the renewal of humanity.

Take the following example, an Easter sermon preached before King James in which he connects the resurrection to the whole of the Christian story, especially the incarnation, and outlines the way humanity and divinity are now one and joined for ever in Christ. Andrewes uses as his guiding idea, and as a refrain, a Latin verse from Psalm 2, the set psalm for Easter Day: 'this day I have begotten you'. The language is rather gendered, reflecting his context and his time, but the imagery is extraordinary, culminating in allusion to one of Andrewes' most beloved Bible verses, 2 Peter 1.4, with its description of the 'theosis' discussed earlier – the Eastern Christian notion of the way humanity comes to share in the very life of God through Christ's birth, death and resurrection, and by our own commitment to the life of prayer. Try reading it slowly, and aloud, to sense the grandeur of the prose and to overcome the strangeness of some of the expression.

But where is Easter Day, what is become of it all this while? For methinks, all the time we are thus about Father and Son, and taking our nature and becoming one of us, it should be Christmas by this, and not Easter as it is; that this is a meeter text one would think for that feast, and that now it comes out of season.

Not a whit. It is Christ that speaketh, and He never speaketh but in season; never but to the purpose, never but on the right day. A brotherhood we grant, was begun at Christmas by his birth, as upon that day, for 'lo then was He born.' But so was He now also at Easter; born then too, and after a better manner born. His resurrection was a second birth, Easter a second Christmas. *Hodie genui Te,*[66] as true of this day as of that. The Church appointeth for the first Psalm this day the second Psalm, the Psalm of *hodie genui Te.* The Apostle saith expressly, when He rose from the dead, then was *hodie genui Te* fulfilled in Him, verified of Him (Acts 13.33). Then He was 'God's first begotten from the dead' (Col. 1.18). And upon this latter birth doth the brotherhood of this day depend.

There was then a new begetting this day. And if a new begetting, a new paternity, and fraternity both. By the *hodie genui Te* of Christmas, how soon He was born of the Virgin's womb He became our brother, sin except, subject to all our infirmities; so to mortality, and even to death itself. And by death that brotherhood has been dissolved, but for this day's rising. By the *hodie genui Te* of Easter, as soon as He was born again of the womb of the grave, He begins a new brotherhood, founds a new fraternity straight; adopts us we see anew again by His [words to us, 'my brothers'], and thereby He that was 'first-begotten from the dead' (Rom. 8.29), becomes 'first-begotten' in this respect 'among many brethren' (Rev. 1.5). Before He was ours, now we are His. That was by the mother's side – so, He ours. This is by the Father's side – so, we His. But half-brothers before, never of whole blood till now. Now by Father and mother both, brothers of one Father, fully brothers, we cannot be more.

. . . So mortal He was, when He ours; but now when we His, He is immortal, and we brethren to Him in that state, the state of immortality. Brethren before, but not to [ascend with him]; now to [ascend with him] and all. Death was in danger to have dissolved that, but death hath now no power on Him, or on this; this shall never be in danger of being dissolved any more. That without this is nothing.

. . . I [speak of] the partaking of His divine nature, to give us full and perfect assurance, as He took our flesh and became our Brother, flesh of our flesh then, so He gives us His flesh, that we may become His brethren, flesh of His flesh, now; and gives it upon this day, the very day of our adoption into this fraternity.[67]

Or consider the next example, a passage from a Pentecost sermon delivered at court in 1610, in which Andrewes' unlikely choice of focus is the word 'if' in John 14.15: 'If ye love me, keep my commandments.' Using again his technique of connecting the particular festival or season at hand with the whole narrative arc of the Christian story, he squeezes from that 'if' more meaning and enquiry than might have been thought possible.

To begin then with the first; 'If ye love Me'. 'Love' is not so fit here, as 'if' is unfitting. For 'if' is as if there were some if, some doubt in the matter; whereof, God forbid there should be any. It would be without 'if'. Thus rather: 'forasmuch as you love Me, keep My Commandments'. That they and we love Him, I trust, shall not need to be put as a hypothesis; 'seeing He is so well worthy of our love', that we to blame, if we endure any 'if', any question to be made of it.

It grieveth me to stand long on this condition, to make an *if* of it at Pentecost. Take the feasts all along, and see if by every one of them 'it' be not put past 'if'. Christmas-day: for us and for our love, He 'became flesh', that we might love Him, because like us He took our nature on Him. New year's-day: 'knowing no sin, He was made sin for us', sealed the bond with first drops of His blood, wherewith the debt of our sin light upon Him. Candlemas-day: He was presented in the Temple, offered as a live oblation for us, that so the obedience of His whole life might be ours. Good Friday: made a slain sacrifice on the cross, that we might be redeemed by the benefit of His death. Easter-day: opened us the gate of life, 'as the first-fruits of them' that rise again. Ascension-day: opened us the gate of Heaven; thither, 'our forerunner entered', to prepare a place for us. And this day seals up all by giving us seisin [i.e. possession] of all He hath done for us, by His Spirit sent down upon earth. And after all this, come ye in with 'If ye love me'? Shall we not strike out 'if', and make the condition absolute? Shall we not to St. Paul's 'if', 'If any man love not the Lord Jesus, let him be [accursed]', all say let him be so?

'If we love them that love us, what singular thing do we, since the very Publicans do the like'? That if our love be but as the Publican's, there would be no 'if' made of it, for He loved us. And not because we loved Him, but He loved us first.

. . . Specially, since His love was not little, but such as St. John makes 'see how great love'. How great? So, as none greater. 'For greater love hath no man than this, to give his life for his friends'. No man greater but He, for His was beyond. To give His life, is but to die any sort of death; but 'by the death of the Cross', to die as He died, that is more. And for such as were His friends is much, but 'while we were yet sinners' is a great deal more. And yet is it 'If'? Put it to the Prophet's question, 'What should He have done', and add to it, if ye will, 'What should He have suffered'? What should He have done, and what suffered? If He did it not, if He suffered not, make an 'if' of His love; but if He did both, out with it.

But the Publican will be the Publican, and the world the world, their love is mercenary sale ware; no profit, no love. To take away that 'if', even thither He will follow us, and apply Himself to that. And if we will make port-sale [i.e. an auction] of our love, and let it go by, Who gives more? He will outbid all. All, by the last word, 'to Eternity'. For whatsoever we may have here, if it were a kingdom, it is not forever. But this 'Comforter' that 'shall abide with us', is but a pledge of that bliss and kingdom of His wherein we shall abide with Him eternally. Let any offer more for our love, and carry it.[68]

Perhaps T. S. Eliot's most significant contribution to making Andrewes' work better known was his quoting of one of his Christmas sermons in a poem of his own, 'The Journey of the Magi', written in the year of his conversion to Anglicanism. Eliot opens the poem by putting into the mouth of one of the visitors from the East to Bethlehem the words of Andrewes, three centuries earlier. The sermon itself used Matthew's description of the arrival of these exotic guests, that first Christmas, to compare their enthusiasm to *act* on the signs they saw and the faith they produced with the inertia of many others. These Magi, Andrewes pointed out, demonstrated a far more lively and engaged attitude to following their faith wherever it led, than do most Christians. He thus offers us an early piece of interreligious theology, centuries ahead of some modern insights.

It is not commended to stand gazing up to heaven too long; not on Christ Himself ascending, much less on His star. For they sat not still gazing on the star. Their 'we have seen' begat 'we are come'; their seeing made them come, but many a wild and weary step they made before they could come to say, 'Lo, here we are come'; come, and at our journey's end. To look a little on it. In this, their coming we consider, first the distance of the place they came from. It was not hard by as the shepherds, but a step to Bethlehem over the fields; this was riding many a hundred miles, and cost them many a day's journey. Secondly, we consider the way that they came, if it be pleasant, or plain and easy; for if it be, it is so much the better. This was nothing pleasant, for through deserts, all the way waste and desolate. Nor, secondly, easy either; for over the rocks and crags of both Arabias, especially Petrea, their journey lay. Yet if safe – but it was not, but exceeding dangerous, as lying through the midst of the 'black tents, of Kedar', a nation of thieves, and, cut-throats; to pass over the hills of robbers, infamous then and infamous to this day. No passing without great troop or convoy. Last we consider the time of their coming, the season of the year. It was no summer progress. A cold coming they had of it at this time of the year, just the worst time of the year to take a journey, and specially a long journey in. The ways deep, the weather sharp, the days short, the sun farthest off in 'the very dead of winter'. 'We are come', if that be one, 'we are come', we are now come, come at this time, that sure is another.

And these difficulties they overcame, of a wearisome, irksome, troublesome, dangerous, unseasonable journey; and for all this they came. And came it, cheerfully and quickly, as appeareth by the speed they made. It was but 'we have seen', 'we are come', with them; 'they saw' and 'they came'; they no sooner saw, but they set out presently. So as upon the first appearing of the star, as it might be last night, they knew it was Balaam's star; it called them away, they made ready straight to begin their journey this morning. A sign they were highly conceited of His birth, believed some great matter of it, that they took all these pains, made all this haste that they might be there to worship Him with all the possible speed they could. Sorry for nothing so much as that they could not be there soon enough, with the very first, to do it even this day, the day of His birth. All considered, so there is more in 'we are come' than shows at the first sight. It was not for nothing it was said in the first verse, 'behold there came'; their coming hath a 'behold' in it, well deserves it.

And we, what should we have done? Sure these men of the East shall rise in judgement against the men of the West, that is us, and their faith against ours in this point. With them it was but 'we have seen', 'we are come'; with us it would have been but 'we are coming' at most. Our fashion is, to see and see again, before we stir a foot, specially if it be to the worship of Christ. Come such a journey at such a time? No; but fairly have put it off to the spring of the year, till the days longer, and the ways fairer, and the weather warmer, till better travelling to Christ. Our Epiphany would sure have fallen in Easter week at the soonest.[69]

Lancelot Andrewes did not, in the end, attain the highest position in the Church of England for which many thought him the obvious and best-equipped candidate. When Richard Bancroft died in 1610, George Abbot succeeded him as Archbishop, and went on to demonstrate his own deficiencies in the role. Abbot's views were reliably Calvinist, however, and he probably in the event seemed a safer choice than Andrewes, whose theology, though gorgeously expressed and beautifully couched in the rolling prose of his court sermons, was less mainstream at times and in some areas. Nevertheless, whatever his own position in the debates and divisions of his own time, Andrewes' influence was immense. Nor was he himself a divisive figure: always secure in his own attitude, he sought to foster a shared sense of purpose between and among all Christians. Building his appeal on the massive scholarship he had cultivated, he saw the marks of catholicity beyond the immediate confines of his own formulations and understanding; unlike so many others in the Reformation, he did not seek to frame his own belief as the only possible interpretation of Christian faith and practice. Ironically, given some of the claims made for him much later by people like Eliot, the only group he did fiercely resist were Catholics: although in some areas closer to their theology, his sermons on the anniversaries of their plots against England grew sometimes intemperately fierce.

When he died in 1626, just a little after the coronation of King Charles I, Andrewes could not have foreseen the chaos and civil war into which his beloved nation would soon be thrown. Although himself of the 'Arminian' party within the Church of England – delighting in Christ's Real Presence in the Eucharist; believing that worship and the space in which it took place should be beautiful, as befitting the God it adored; resisting the extremes of Calvinist theology and placing some emphasis on the need for humanity to co-operate with God and thus move towards divinity – he exhibited a peaceful, reconciling spirit of wise inclusion in the Church's life that was appallingly lacking in his later colleagues, including Archbishop William Laud. Although he never bequeathed a weighty systematic treatise to posterity, like his contemporary Richard Hooker, his influence is just as great, if more subtle. In his drawing together of ancient sources, Eastern and Western, his dynamic evocation of the power of God's life at work in humanity to make us whole in love, his passionate advocacy for the beauty of holiness and his efforts to widen the circle of Anglican belonging and identity, Lancelot Andrewes lives on in the best of the tradition he loved and helped to shape. Belonging now to no party or faction, he has influenced Methodism quite as much as Tractarianism, personal devotion as much as corporate worship, and the discipleship of 'ordinary' Christians as much as the public faith of monarchs.

We end with a glimpse of the private man. Andrewes' *Private Prayers*, written in Latin and for his own use and devotion, have been published in a variety of editions and translations. A vast and yet seamless compendium of biblical and patristic sources, they are yet all his own and breathe his spirit. In their voice we get closest to this devout and holy man, called upon to exercise high and responsible office and yet never neglectful of his prayers any more than he was of his reading and reflection. The learned mind of the scholar, the prayerful soul of a Puritan and the generous heart of an Arminian Anglican are all on display here, and these passages still speak today of the everlasting value of all three.

An Act of Adoration

O God the Father of heaven,
    who hast marvellously created the world out of nothing,
    who dost govern and uphold heaven and earth with thy
    power,
    who didst deliver thine only-begotten for us unto
    death:
O God the Son, Redeemer of the world,
    who didst will to be incarnate of a virgin, who hast
    washed us from our sins by thy precious blood,
    who rising from the dead didst ascend victorious to
    heaven:
O God the Holy Ghost, the Comforter,
    who didst descend upon Jesus in the form of a dove,
    who coming upon the apostles didst appear in fiery
    tongues,
    who dost visit and confirm with thy grace the hearts
    of the saints:
O sacred, highest, eternal, blissful, blessed Trinity,
    always to be praised, yet always unspeakable:
        O Father good,
        O Son loving,
        O Spirit kind,
            whose majesty is unspeakable,
            whose power is incomparable,
            whose goodness is inestimable:
            whose work is life,
            whose love is grace,
            whose contemplation is glory:

Deity, Divinity, Unity, Trinity:
   Thee I worship, Thee I call upon,
       with the whole affection of my heart I bless
       now and for evermore.

A Prayer for Our Country

Of the fruits of the earth and of the fullness thereof:
   bless our ingathering,
   make peace in our borders,
   fill us with the flour of wheat,
   satisfy our poor with bread,
   make fast the bars of our gates,
   bless our children within us;
   clothe our enemies with shame;
   bestow temperate weather,
   grant the fruits of the earth;
   drive away fleshly desires;
   restore health to the sick,
   grant restoration to the fallen,
   to voyagers and wayfarers,
      a prosperous journey and a haven of safety;
   to the afflicted, joy;
   to the oppressed, relief;
   to captives grant liberty:
   sanity of mind,
   soundness of body,
   strength of faith,
   security of hope,
   defence of salvation.

LANCELOT ANDREWES

Conclusion of Thanksgiving

O Lord, I am not worthy of the least of all the mercies
and of all the truth which thou has showed unto thy
servant:
and what can I say more unto Thee?
    for thou, Lord, my Lord, knowest thy servant.
Who am I, O Lord, thy servant, and what is my house,
    that Thou shouldest look upon such a dead dog as I
    am,
    that Thou hast loved me hitherto?
What reward shall I give unto the Lord
    for all the benefits that He hath done unto me?
What thanks can we render to God again
    for all the joy wherewith we joy before Him?
Thou that hast vouchsafed unto me, O Lord, on this
holy day and at this hour to lift up
    my soul and to praise Thee and to offer the glory that
    is due unto Thee:
Do Thou thyself, O Lord, accept of my soul this spiritual
sacrifice, and receiving it unto
    Thee on to thy spiritual altar, vouchsafe in requital
    thereof to send upon me the grace
    of thy most holy Spirit.
Visit me in thy goodness:
    forgive me every sin, as well voluntary as involuntary:
deliver me from eternal punishments; yea, and from all
the distresses of this world:
transform my thoughts unto piety,
    hallow my spirit, soul and body,
and grant me to worship and to please Thee
    in piety and holiness of life,
            even unto the last end of life.
Now unto Him that is able to do exceedingly abundantly
above all that we ask or think,

according to the power that worketh in us:
unto Him be glory in the Church in Christ throughout all ages, world without end.

My soul shall be satisfied even as it were with marrow and fatness,
> when my mouth praiseth Thee with joyful lips.

For the Quick and the Dead

Thou which art Lord at once of the living and of the dead;
Whose are we whom the present world yet holdeth in the flesh;
Whose are they withal whom, unclothed of the body,
the world to come hath even now received:
give to the living mercy and grace,
> to the dead rest and light perpetual:

give to the Church truth and peace,
> to us sinners penitence and pardon.[70]

9

'Make me Thine': George Herbert

I know the ways of learning; both the head
And pipes that feed the press, and make it run;
What reason hath from nature borrowed,
Or of it self, like a good housewife, spun
In laws and policy; what the stars conspire,
What willing nature speaks, what forc'd by fire;
Both th' old discoveries, and the new-found seas,
The stock and surplus, cause and history:
All these stand open, or I have the keys:
                              Yet I love thee.

I know the ways of honour, what maintains
The quick returns of courtesy and wit:
In vies of favours whether party gains,
When glory swells the heart, and mouldeth it
To all expressions both of hand and eye,
Which on the world a true-love knot may tie,
And bear the bundle, wheresoe're it goes:
How many drams of spirit there must be
To sell my life unto my friends or foes:
                              Yet I love thee.

I know the ways of pleasure, the sweet strains,
The lullings and the relishes of it;
The propositions of hot blood and brains;
What mirth and music mean; what love and wit
Have done these twenty hundred years, and more:
I know the projects of unbridled store:

My stuff is flesh, not brass; my senses live,
And grumble oft, that they have more in me
Than he that curbs them, being but one to five:
        Yet I love thee.

I know all these, and have them in my hand:
Therefore not seeled, but with open eyes
I fly to thee, and fully understand
Both the main sale, and the commodities;
And at what rate and price I have thy love;
With all the circumstances that may move:
Yet through the labyrinths, not my grovelling wit,
But thy silk twist let down from heav'n to me,
Did both conduct and teach me, how by it
        To climb to thee.[71]

This poem, 'The Pearl', with its allusions to Matthew 13, may come close to describing the inner life of one of the English Reformation's most elusive and yet most beloved men. George Herbert's biographers, taking their tone from the first, Izaak Walton in 1670, have often asserted a rather romantic idea of his life's course, and certainly his decision ultimately to abandon academic and courtly promise in order to end his days the rector of a small country parish is a striking one. But as the poem hints at, rather than this being a sudden moment of conversion and clarity, the first 30 years of Herbert's short life were seasoned and even characterized by a continual sense of struggle and of search. Recent re-evaluations of the dating of his poetry have also yielded us insights into this struggle by showing that some of the poems now regarded as the greatest were in fact the product of his years before parish ministry. The process by which George Herbert, aristocrat, scholar, orator, Member of Parliament and fellow of Trinity College, Cambridge became the resident of the rectory at Bemerton was indeed a slow climb – or, in the eyes of the world perhaps, a long descent. In any case, he came to detect the silken thread of divine love running throughout it.

Born in 1593 to a well-to-do family with noble and even royal connections, George Herbert began his life in Montgomery, Wales. His father Richard died when George was just three, and his bond with his mother Magdalen was especially close, perhaps partly as a result of this traumatic childhood bereavement. Reliant on the kindness and hospitality of family and friends, Magdalen took the family to Oxford for a while and then to London. She was a remarkable woman: cultured, intellectual, witty and lively. She became friends with John Donne, whose later career, both as a priest and as a poet, made him influential on her son's career also. The two remained in contact until her death in 1627; the memorial sermon Donne preached at her funeral celebrated her 'holy cheerfulness' in terms that emphasized the depth of his own devotion to her and his gratitude for her generosity and friendship.

The move to London meant that Magdalen needed to find a local school for her talented son. In 1604, aged 11, George began studies at Westminster School. The Dean of Westminster, Lancelot Andrewes, himself took a very engaged approach to the life of the Abbey's school and personally tutored and encouraged the boys. Unsurprisingly, Andrewes thus became a key influence on George Herbert, a boy whose gifts he noticed and nurtured. It's possible to see in Herbert's later poetry an ability to wring every last meaning out of a word or idea, or to play with metaphors in a variety of scintillating ways, that is similar to that in Andrewes' sermons. Indeed, before Herbert's poetry ever won him any attention, he was himself a famed public speaker and orator, at the highest levels of the land, and in his capacity for this his mentor's influence must also have been strong. Although the Dean's promotion to the bishopric of Chichester came just a year after Herbert's admission to the school, they remained in touch.

George Herbert's early life followed the natural progression of young men like him: he went to Trinity College, Cambridge in 1609 to begin his studies, little knowing how pivotal a place

Cambridge was to be for him in his rise towards an illustrious career, the cultivation of his poetic gifts and his eventual disappointment with received wisdom on what made for an accomplished life. In the same year his mother took a new husband, Sir John Danvers. Danvers was half his bride's age and a contemporary of George's elder brother Edward, something rather more unusual and even more likely to cause gossip then than it would be now, but their marriage proved immensely happy, despite some initial reserve from his relatives. George was immensely fond of his young stepfather, enjoyed his visits home and developed a relationship with him that sustained him both emotionally and materially, even after his mother's death.

Herbert's intellect and insight guaranteed him an easy path to success in a place like Cambridge; he graduated BA in 1613 and MA in 1616, having been elected a minor fellow of Trinity. He became a tutor, as Praelector in Rhetoric, and was, finally, appointed the University's Public Orator in 1619. In this role he was the public voice of the university on ceremonial and great occasions, and he fulfilled it with eminent success, winning praise for his facility with language and his ability to hold his hearers' attention. As his brother Edward took up his own new role as Ambassador to France in the same year, it must have seemed as though the family was coming into a period of achievement, stability and even renown.

Other thoughts were stirring in George Herbert though, and perhaps had been ever since his earliest days. The idea of ordination, which would not have been strange for a young man of his position and ability, seems to have been one that refused to lie down. Maybe his exposure to the genius of Lancelot Andrewes had lit a spark in his imagination, and he saw a way more usefully to join his talents to some greater purpose than speechifying. Maybe his don's life in Cambridge simply felt too far removed from what he took to be edifying and profitable ways to spend one's life. In any case it was certainly this idea of 'usefulness' that dominated his agonized reflections on the path his life should take. In 1623 he fulfilled a duty by taking up the parliamentary seat of Montgomeryshire: perhaps not so much an indication that he was testing a political career as evidence of familial responsibility, given his birth. Nevertheless it was a moment in which an even more illustrious career in government presented itself for his consideration. Herbert absolutely refused it. Within weeks of finishing his parliamentary term, in 1624, he was ordained deacon, under special measures.

Something of the tension and anxiety in the prevarication he was undergoing reveals itself in his poetry about priesthood, probably dating from these years. Herbert took a lofty view of the role of priest, with its authority to absolve sin and dispense communion, which he understood to contain the very life of God. His own sense of unworthiness and sin horrified him, and he questioned and second-guessed his own exploration of this possibility. Yet for all that, the sense that priestly ordination might be his own calling wouldn't let him alone; he resolved to cultivate his own prayer life, wait and see how divine providence might manifest itself. After all, if clay can be refined and fired into fine china, perhaps even frail humans can make priests:

> Blest Order, which in power dost so excel,
> That with th' one hand thou liftest to the sky,
> And with the other throwest down to hell
> In thy just censures; fain would I draw nigh,
> Fain put thee on, exchanging my lay-sword
>   For that of th' holy word.

> But thou art fire, sacred and hallow'd fire;
> And I but earth and clay: should I presume
> To wear thy habit, the severe attire
> My slender compositions might consume.
> I am both foul and brittle; much unfit
>   To deal in holy Writ.

TO GAIN AT HARVEST

Yet have I often seen, by cunning hand
And force of fire, what curious things are made
Of wretched earth. Where once I scorn'd to stand,
That earth is fitted by the fire and trade
Of skilful artists, for the boards of those
           Who make the bravest shows.

But since those great ones, be they ne're so great,
Come from the earth, from whence those vessels come;
So that at once both feeder, dish, and meat
Have one beginning and one final sum:
I do not greatly wonder at the sight,
           If earth in earth delight.

But th' holy men of God such vessels are,
As serve him up, who all the world commands:
When God vouchsafeth to become our fare,
Their hands convey him, who conveys their hands.
O what pure things, most pure must those things be,
           Who bring my God to me!

Wherefore I dare not, I, put forth my hand
To hold the Ark, although it seem to shake
Through th' old sins and new doctrines of our land.
Only, since God doth often vessels make
Of lowly matter for high uses meet,
           I throw me at his feet.

There will I lie, until my Maker seek
For some mean stuff whereon to show his skill:
Then is my time. The distance of the meek
Doth flatter power. Lest good come short of ill
In praising might, the poor do by submission
           What pride by opposition.[72]

During the latter half of the 1620s, Herbert was probably not much at Cambridge, although still holding both his fellowship and the post of Public Orator. His spiritual pilgrimage was mirrored in a quite itinerant lifestyle, spending his time successively with members of his family and with friends, writing poetry and, through prayer and reflection, discerning his future. It was also nurtured through one very significant friendship, with a man whose life and whose emerging sense of vocation was in many ways echoing his own. George Herbert and Nicholas Ferrar had been soulmates since undergraduate days. After a rather more distinguished parliamentary career than Herbert's, and following time spent travelling overseas about the business of the family trading interest, the London Virginia Company, Ferrar had a spiritual awakening. It led him to pursue a vocation that many in his own day gravely misunderstood. In 1626 he bought the small manor at Little Gidding in Huntingdonshire and took his extended family with him to undertake a holy experiment. They lived in semi-monastic isolation and prayer, without an official rule of life but maintaining a permanent, prayerful presence in the little abandoned church there, which they renovated. At one level profoundly Anglican, basing its common life on the liturgy of the Book of Common Prayer and a very simple, self-sufficient lifestyle, Ferrar's community attracted the opprobrium of those who saw it as a dangerous reversion to Catholic practices.

The 'freedom from all other affairs' that the Little Gidding community enjoyed, and the depth and richness of its life of prayer, attracted Herbert immeasurably. Given the living of the neighbouring parish of Leighton Bromswold, where he set about rebuilding and reappointing the church although he was not resident in the parish, he visited his old friend more than once. Scrawled on the wall of the parlour were the words: 'He who by a cheerful participation and approbation of that which is good, confirms us in the same, is welcome as a Christian friend.' They were words Herbert delighted to fulfil on his journeys to this remote place and its community, unique in Britain. He also came to share their sense that such a life, in such circumstances, was the pinnacle of human existence: 'this, Lord, is the work of, and this the pleasure of, angels in heaven', the Ferrars are said to have asserted, before marvelling at their good fortune to have been made 'partakers of so high a happiness'.[73] Herbert was captivated, pondering where he might himself establish a similar way of life and cultivate his own spirituality.

Two further and life-altering events probably continued to shape his search: the death of his mother, Magdalen, in 1627, and then his marriage to Jane Danvers in March 1629. Jane was a cousin of his stepfather, perfectly suited to his inclinations, tempers and interests. If his mother's death came as a great blow to him and caused him prolonged grief, we also know from Donne that she had suffered from a long period of depression leading up to it. Judging from his poetry, it seems that her son shared a predisposition to similar difficulties. The uncertainty of his life, his struggle for meaning and purpose in living it, and the loss of those closest to him, as well as a natural inclination to feelings of melancholy and even despair, were surely contributory factors. If we can imagine that Jane's arrival in his life brought him a much-needed companion in such trials, we know that his faith was his main source of consolation in these years of aridity and occasional hopelessness. Take his poem 'The Dawning' as an example:

> Awake sad heart, whom sorrow ever drowns;
>> Take up thine eyes, which feed on earth;
> Unfold thy forehead gather'd into frowns:
>> Thy Saviour comes, and with him mirth:
>>> Awake, awake;
> And with a thankful heart his comforts take.
>> But thou dost still lament, and pine, and cry;
>> And feel his death, but not his victory.
>
> Arise sad heart; if thou does not withstand,
>> Christ's resurrection thine may be:

Do not by hanging down break from the hand,
    Which as it riseth, raiseth thee:
        Arise, arise;
  And with his burial-linen dry thine eyes:
    Christ left his grave-clothes, that we might, when grief
Draws tears, or blood, not want an handkerchief.[74]

Or at the opposite end of the day, the exquisite 'Even-song', a tender tribute to the healing powers of night at the end of days of sorrow, purposelessness and difficulty:

      Blest be the God of love,
  Who gave me eyes, and light, and power this day,
      Both to be busy, and to play.
    But much more blest be God above,
        Who gave me sight alone,
    Which to himself he did deny:
    For when he sees my ways, I die:
But I have got his son, and he hath none.

      What have I brought thee home
  For this thy love? Have I discharg'd the debt,
      Which this day's favour did beget?
    I ran; but all I brought, was foam.
        Thy diet, care, and cost
    Do end in bubbles, balls of wind;
    Of wind to thee whom I have crost,
But balls of wild-fire to my troubled mind.

      Yet still thou goest on,
  And now with darkness closest weary eyes,
      Saying to man, *It doth suffice:*
Henceforth repose; your work is done.
        Thus in thy Ebony box
    Thou dost enclose us, till the day

Put our amendment in our way,
And give new wheels to our disorder'd clocks.

I muse, which shows more love,
The day or night: that is the gale, this th' harbour;
That is the walk, and this the arbour;
Or that the garden, this the grove.
My God, thou art all love.
Not one poor minute scapes thy breast,
But brings a favour from above;
And in this love, more than in bed, I rest.[75]

In one of his most famous verses, 'The Collar', Herbert describes the angrier, most frustrated expression of his own dissatisfaction and uncertainty, the moments in which he felt his whole life pointless and his living a mere sham. Tired of the sometimes exhausting quest for vocation, of being in the 'right' place, even after his ordination, he resolves again to live as he desires, solely for human pleasures:

I struck the board, and cry'd, No more.
I will abroad.
What? Shall I ever sigh and pine?
My lines and life are free; free as the road.
Loose as the wind, as large as store.
Shall I be still in suit?
Have I no harvest but a thorn
To let me blood, and not restore
What I have lost with cordial fruit?
Sure there was wine
Before my sighs did dry it: there was corn
Before my tears did drown it.
Is the year only lost to me?
Have I no bays to crown it?

No flowers, no garlands gay? all blasted?
All wasted?[76]

The poem goes on, its rage and sense of futility building with every line, until the whole thing is brought tumbling down – and the mood dramatically shifted and altered – by the final lines and the gentle epiphany that changes everything and restores perspective:

But as I rav'd and grew more fierce and wild
At every word,
Me thoughts I heard one calling, *Child:*
And I reply'd, *My Lord.*[77]

The end of all this journeying, to misquote T. S. Eliot's own re-action to Little Gidding, was Bemerton, a small parish three miles outside Salisbury. Herbert was appointed priest in 1630 and there he lived out what would be the final three years of his brief life. He finally took priestly orders, in fact, to accept the appointment, which came his way when King Charles I approved it, apparently one among many to be amazed that someone of Herbert's talents would undertake so lowly a task. To Herbert it was anything but. As we have seen, his own resistance to priesthood derived from a weighty sense of the solemnity and responsibility of the office. His friend Arthur Woodnoth recounted a striking story of the night of the new priest's installation, which Izaak Walton faithfully relayed:

When at his induction he was shut into Bemerton Church, being left there alone to toll the bell (as the law requires him), he stayed so much longer than an ordinary time before he returned to those friends that stayed expecting him at the church door, that his friend . . . looked in at the church window, and saw him lie prostrate on the ground before the altar; at which time and place . . . he set some rules to himself for the future manage of his life, and then and there made a vow to labour to keep them.[78]

After so long a period of introspection, prayerful discernment and itinerant uncertainty, acceptance of the duties of priest at Bemerton and the necessary final severing of his connections and duties in Cambridge must have seemed a moment of the greatest consequence.

The manner of Herbert's life as priest, and the content of those rules he forged for himself in solitary prostration in front of his own altar, he laid down for publication in his treatise, *A Priest to the Temple*. Impossibly old-fashioned nowadays, they are easy to scorn;[79] but they emanate his careful, prayerful, compassionate approach to parish ministry, the spirit of which is desirable in any age. They also reflect a vision, which we might hope is not quite dead yet, of the need for clergy to: ensure that their reading and immersion in theological material is assiduous and up to date; pay particular attention to their preaching ministry and to ensure the relevance of their message for their audience; be attentive to the holistic needs of their parishioners and not merely their spiritual lives; be the model of compassion, charity and self-awareness for the whole community; and despise or dismiss none of those in their charge and care, however poor, squalid, deprived or marginal their estate and condition are, 'for both God is there also, and those for whom God died'.

We have no reliable first-hand accounts of Herbert's time as Bemerton's priest. If he lived according to his own handbook, the residents of that place must have felt immensely well cared for by him, even if at times his approach may have seemed a little too 'hands on'. He and Jane enjoyed their close proximity to Wilton House, where his relation William Herbert, the Earl of Pembroke, lived with his family, and to which they regularly repaired. Herbert himself was also grateful for Bemerton's easy access, across the water meadows later made famous by John Constable, to Salisbury, and to the worshipping life of an ancient and great cathedral. Here he joined the congregation several times a week, particularly appreciating choral Evensong. If Walton's *Life* is even remotely accurate in this regard, these were blissfully happy years, surrounded by family, appreciative parishioners, a devoted wife, a sense of being where he needed to be and, at long last, having achieved the resolution of his long discomfort and vocational angst. It is therefore all the more distressing that they ended so abruptly. A month short both of the third anniversary of his appointment to Bemerton and of his fortieth birthday, George Herbert died, on 1 March 1633, probably from tuberculosis.

So far his relationship to the great upheavals and the doctrinal divisions of the English Reformation has not much needed to concern us. In one way George Herbert played no great or defining role in these struggles, neither a bishop nor a published systematic theologian. In another way, though, his influence on the Church of England – and far beyond it – has been immense. Like his boyhood mentor Lancelot Andrewes, his fusion of varied elements into what later came to be seen as 'Anglican' distinctives can be traced through his poetry: a deep love of and saturation in the Scriptures; a mystical preoccupation with a contemplative life; a concern for method and rigour in Christian discipleship; a clear view that 'the beauty of holiness' should be as much evident in the generosity of the individual's life as in spaces for and occasions of public worship. He was equally clear that while he was immeasurably grateful for the necessary renewal in the life of the Church brought about by the Reformation, so much of its 'second tier' contentiousness was simply a kind of individualism, even arrogance, that ought to know better. For the 'debates and fretting jealousies' of his time, as he called them, he had no patience. The striking admixture of all these elements is in evidence in his poem about the spiritual disciplines of Lent: his commitment to spiritual disciplines; devotion to the settled order of the English Church; impatience with the incessant rancour from those unwilling to accept its polity; and his deep compassion for the needs of others.

TO GAIN AT HARVEST

Welcome dear feast of Lent: who loves not thee,
He loves not Temperance, or Authority,
                         But is compos'd of passion.
The Scriptures bid us *fast*; the Church says, *now*:
Give to thy Mother, what thou wouldst allow
                     To ev'ry Corporation.

The humble soul compos'd of love and fear
Begins at home, and lays the burden there,
                     When doctrines disagree.
He says, in things which use hath justly got,
I am a scandal to the Church, and not
                     The Church is so to me . . .

It's true, we cannot reach Christ's forti'th day;
Yet to go part of that religious way . . .
                     Is better than to rest:
We cannot reach our Saviour's purity;
Yet we are bid, *Be holy ev'n as he.*
                     In both let's do our best.

Who goeth in the way which Christ hath gone,
Is much more sure to meet with him, than one
                     That travelleth by-ways:
Perhaps my God, though he be far before,
May turn and take me by the hand, and more:
                     May strengthen my decays.

Yet Lord instruct us to improve our fast
By starving sin and taking such repast,
                     As may our faults control:
That eve'ry man may revel at his door,
Not in his parlour; banqueting the poor,
                     And among those his soul.[80]

Nor were the spiritual disciplines, for George Herbert, all about unpleasantness and mere duty. An essentially gentle man, he spoke of the way he sought his own comfort from the stresses of his existence in prayer and contemplation. The experience of doing so he described in poetry of exquisite beauty and inventiveness. In the next chapter we shall meet the remarkable Thomas Traherne, but language like that in Herbert's 'Prayer' warrants a place among the English mystics for its author as well:

Prayer the Church's banquet, Angels' age,
    God's breath in man returning to his birth,
    The soul in paraphrase, heart in pilgrimage,
The Christians plummet sounding heav'n and earth;
Engine against th' Almighty, sinners' tower,
    Reversed thunder, Christ-side-piercing spear,
    The six-days-world transposing in an hour,
A kind of tune, which all things hear and fear;
Softness, and peace, and joy, and love, and bliss,
    Exalted Manna, gladness of the best,
    Heaven in ordinary, mean well drest,
The milky way, the bird of Paradise,
    Church-bells beyond the stars heard, the soul's blood,
    The land of spices; something understood.[81]

The lineaments of the character of Herbert's God, though, and the compelling and yet direct way he describes him are his greatest claim on posterity's gratitude. Out of the contended claims of the Reformation his poetry reflects his own experience of a God of infinite grace and unutterable, transformative love: a God who weeps and mourns and rejoices with humanity and whose gifts towards creation are unceasing and spring from an abundance of generous delight. It is in the enjoyment of the blessings and benefits of this God that Herbert posits his hope for renewal and reconciliation on earth, as human beings learn that the ways of God might transfigure their own deficient patterns of behaviours and cycles of revenge. Here he is, in 'Discipline':

Throw away thy rod,
Throw away thy wrath:
   O my God,
Take the gentle path.

For my heart's desire
Unto thine is bent:
   I aspire
To a full consent.

Not a word or look
I affect to own,
   But by book,
And thy book alone.

Though I fail, I weep:
Though I halt in pace,
   Yet I creep
To the throne of grace.

Then let wrath remove;
Love will do the deed:
   For with love
Stony hearts will bleed.

Love is swift of foot;
Love's a man of war,
   And can shoot,
And can hit from far.

Who can scape his bow?
That which wrought on thee,

Brought thee low,
Needs must work on me.

Throw away thy rod;
Though man frailties hath,
Thou art God
Throw away thy wrath.[82]

The full power and utter wonder of this divine love, and its effects on guilty, clenched human nature, Herbert famously celebrated in his third poem called 'Love', with its depiction of a rich banquet, spread by a gentle deity before an unwilling human guest. Endlessly quoted and anthologized, it perhaps needs no further repetition here, except to record its massive impact on all subsequent generations of English-speaking Christians. In one way it is a Lutheran poem through and through – a celebration of the sheer, surprising way divine grace changes everything and upturns human standards of wisdom and judgement. In another way it possesses an optimism about the transformative, even sanctifying possibilities of this grace in a human life that feels fresh and exciting. It is small wonder that later Anglicans, Evangelicals and Catholics alike found it such an irresistible glimpse of the gospel's power. In similar vein, Herbert evinced the atonement made possible by Christ in language that drew on the Gospels' language of redemption and the mystical imagery of Mother Julian of Norwich and made them both somehow his own in a miracle of compressed theology. This is 'Redemption':

Having been tenant long to a rich Lord,
Not thriving, I resolved to be bold,
And make a suit unto him, to afford
A new small-rented lease, and cancel th' old.
In heaven at his manor I him sought:
They told me there, that he was lately gone
About some land, which he had dearly bought

Long since on earth, to take possession.
I straight return'd, and knowing his great birth,
    Sought him accordingly in great resorts;
    In cities, theatres, gardens, parks, and courts;
At length I heard a ragged noise and mirth
    Of thieves and murderers: there I him espied
    Who straight, *Your suit is granted*, said, and died.[83]

Knowing he was dying, George Herbert made arrangements for his poetry to be sent to his oldest friend and most trusted counsellor. The ambition of his youth, appropriate given his talents and soon gratified in his illustrious career at Cambridge, had long since dissipated. But still, Herbert had a sense that, after his death at least, this manuscript collection of verses might find an audience. An intensely private man, the intimate nature of the way the poems revealed his inner life would have made him resistant to any efforts to publish while he lived. Ironically, his natural humility also blinded him to the fact that this was probably the greatest collection of religious poetry in the English language, unlikely ever to be surpassed. Receiving the poems in Little Gidding, however, Nicholas Ferrar was under no such illusions. The scale and depth of his friend's work was revelatory, even to him. In any case there was no doubt about whether to publish, and the book appeared within the year. Ferrar's judgement proved impeccable. By the time of Isaak Walton's biography in 1670, *The Temple* – as Ferrar had named the collection – was into its tenth printing. Herbert was something of a celebrity and had achieved a fame quite beyond anything he could ever have imagined as Public Orator of Cambridge University, Member of Parliament for Montgomeryshire or even a minister of the Crown.

These were not, in any case, the distinctions he came to recognize as ones worth coveting. With a clarity of insight and a disciplined self-awareness remarkable in any age, Herbert had seen through the fool's gold offered by the world around him, and longed instead for the alchemy of faith, of seeing God 'in ordinary' and transforming even the most mundane task with a heavenly aspiration: 'for that which God doth touch and own/Cannot for less be told'. Elsewhere he expressed his life's governing desire with even more economy:

> Thou that hast giv'n so much to me,
> Give one thing more, a grateful heart.[84]

Or in a mystical encomium to the saving possibilities of contemplation and unitive prayer, he begged, in 'Clasping of Hands':

> Lord, thou art mine, and I am thine,
> If mine I am: and thine much more,
> Than I or ought, or can be mine.
> Yet to be thine, doth me restore;
> So that again I now am mine,
> And with advantage mine the more.
> Since this being mine, brings with it thine,
> And thou with me doth thee restore.
>   If I without thee would be mine,
>   I neither should be mine nor thine.
>
> Lord, I am thine, and thou art mine:
> So mine thou art, that something more
> I may presume thee mine, than thine.
> For thou didst suffer to restore
> Not thee, but me, and to be mine:
> And with advantage mine the more
> Since thou in death wast none of thine,
> Yet then as mine didst me restore.
>   O be mine still! Still make me thine!
>   Or rather make no Thine and Mine![85]

The same year that Herbert died, William Laud was appointed the new Archbishop of Canterbury. As Bishop of London he had approved Herbert's appointment to Bemerton. In many ways their sensibilities in religious matters were rather similar. They were not similar in temperament. Herbert's eirenic and generous ecclesiology found few echoes in Laud's increasingly stubborn and unyielding approach to his office, driven on and exacerbated by the folly and wilful ignorance of King Charles I. England was on a path to a civil war whose causes were partly religious, just as the relative stability of the early century and the reconciling efforts of King James had seemed to be bearing fruit. Herbert would have been horrified by the war and would surely have grieved its beginning – and its very human causes – very deeply. He could not have been more opposed to the kind of thoughtless and implacable narrowness that characterized all sides at different times during that costly conflict.

He would also probably have questioned both sides about their aims and ambitions. For the rector of Bemerton had come to a very clear sense of the proper end and aim of a human life. He expressed it once by using Paul's words to the church in Colossae, spread throughout one of his compositions. He did so in words that raise the reader's thoughts literally to the heavens, via a reflection on the sun's progress through the sky. It offers a reminder, in the words of Jesus, to set one's heart on that which cannot fade or perish. In the ultimate calculation of his own life, at any rate, George Herbert knew the value of his own advice.

Colossians 3.3: *Our life is hid with Christ in God*

My words and thoughts do both express this notion,
That *Life* hath with the sun a double motion.
The first *Is* straight, and our diurnal friend,
The other *Hid*, and doth obliquely bend.
One life is wrapt *In* flesh, and tends to earth.
The other winds towards *Him*, whose happy birth

Taught me to live here so, *That* still one eye
Should aim and shoot at that which *Is* on high:
Quitting with daily labour all *My* pleasure,
To gain at harvest an eternal *Treasure*.[86]

10

Felicity and Desire: Thomas Traherne

About 20 years ago, a friend of mine with whom I shared a love of classical music was introducing me to some of the lesser-known but unjustly neglected corners of twentieth-century British composition. He put a disc into the player and I was immediately transported by a sumptuous, ravishing string melody of great and expressive beauty. The opening movement was followed by another in which a tenor voice began to sing these arresting words:

> Will you see the infancy of this sublime and celestial greatness? I was a stranger, which at my entrance into the world was saluted and surrounded with innumerable joys: my knowledge was divine. I was entertained like an angel with the works of God in their splendour and glory. Heaven and Earth did sing my Creator's praises, and could not make more melody to Adam than to me. Certainly Adam in Paradise had not more sweet and curious apprehensions of the world than I. All appeared new, and strange at first, inexpressibly rare and delightful and beautiful. All things were spotless and pure and glorious.[87]

The music itself was 'glorious', in fact, and I couldn't believe it wasn't more widely known and performed. But the words: something about them caught my imagination and my heart, with their innocence and insight, their evocation of childhood and of the goodness and grace of a loving God who delights in

Creation, their extraordinary vision of all that is good being a generous gift to all of us who enjoy this world.

The music was by Gerald Finzi, and it was *Dies Natalis*, a work he slowly completed over two decades and published in 1939, on the eve of war. Those unforgettable words, my friend informed me, were by Thomas Traherne, from his collection *Centuries of Meditations*. Like Finzi, he had lived through a devastating war. They also died on the same day, 27 September, 282 years apart. As I began to investigate further, it soon became clear that Finzi's attraction to Traherne was one I shared and indeed was slowly expanding more widely. We know little of his life and biography, but his luminous, mystical, glorious writings are in a class of their own, one of the greatest literary achievements in England in the seventeenth century, and one of the most original theological and poetic voices of the period too. We end this collection by encountering a glimpse of his memorable evocation of the goodness of God and the task of humanity. It may be that without the process of the English Reformation we should have been denied Traherne's original genius. It is one reason to be grateful for it, despite all its upheaval and division.

Thomas Traherne was born and formed amid the English Civil War. The causes of the war were complex and its course was long. Without the careful handling of a monarch like James I, the divisions the Reformation had created and left exposed in English religious life were always likely to widen and become more dangerous. During William Laud's tenure as Archbishop of Canterbury that was exactly what happened. His unyielding, unseeing insistence on his own policy, combined with King Charles I's often cavalier – no pun intended – disregard for good sense, diplomacy or caution in his growing closeness to Roman Catholicism, simply fostered and furthered the alarming growth of the country's difference over its national Church and over what form the practice of the faith should take. It was one highly toxic ingredient in the lethal mix which, by the early 1640s, led to a war between Royalist and Parliamentary forces, a war eventually won by the Parliamentarians. The regicide of 1649 was a moment of horror for many, but became imperative in the eyes of parliamentary leaders if peace was ever to be restored.

The Protectorate of 1649–60 proved to be a searing experience for many English people too, as the nation finally tasted some of the effects of the Puritan policies, enacted in parishes all over the land. In the end it was no more unifying than had been the episcopal government of the Elizabethan Settlement. Even more worryingly, these were years of profound and alarming political instability, as parliament after parliament fell apart and Cromwell experimented with just about every form of rule in a chaotic decade, including the bizarre theocracy of the 'Barebone's Parliament' in 1653, which took its nickname from the member for the City of London, a Puritan called Praise-God Barebone. The parliament's members included some of seventeenth-century England's religious 'lunatic fringe', the so-called Fifth Monarchists who interpreted biblical prophecy in such a way as to see eschatological significance in current politics. In fairness their spiritual descendants are still with us, but the parliament was widely ridiculed and utterly insupportable. Its dissolution led directly to the effective creation of a military dictatorship under Cromwell as Lord Protector.

During this time everything rested on Cromwell's charisma, personal authority and ruthless exercise of power. He perpetrated acts of extraordinary barbarity in Ireland, in part driven by his own visceral anti-Catholic views. But he also exercised a far more tolerant policy towards Jews, who had been driven out of England under previous governments. His plans for the Church of England were implemented by a new rigour in ensuring and enforcing soundness of doctrine and teaching in parish ministers and schoolteachers alike, ejecting any whose views did not conform to the kind of Evangelical Puritanism favoured by the Protector. It was all a fascinating experiment, and a far cry from the former moderation of the Jacobean years. Ultimately, however, although possessed of enormous gifts, and a man of deep though sometimes inscrutable faith, Cromwell could not establish long-term security for the nation's life. His son Richard succeeded him as Protector but could not command support. The centre could not hold. In 1660 the monarchy was restored and with it the episcopal Church of England. Charles II returned in triumph from France. What had seemed to many Puritans the moment of their victory would become merely a temporary hiatus in the long and tortured unfolding of the English Reformation.

Thomas Traherne's life is a fascinating one, in part because it unfolded against this very background and because his own commitments and convictions seem to have shifted against it. Born in Hereford, probably in 1637, his early influences and affinities seem to have been Puritan. Raised in comparative poverty, the son of a shoemaker, his mother died when he was very young. Thomas and his brother Philip were then sent to a wet nurse a few miles outside of Hereford to be fed and nourished. Hereford's strategic location on the borders of England and Wales, as well as its surrounding farmland, made it a key location during the Civil War, and a vital city to occupy.

Thomas's earliest memories of political life would thus have been of the vicissitudes to which his home town was subject during these years, the years of his childhood, as it changed hands multiple times between rival forces and also found itself ravaged and its resources ransacked by troops needing shelter and sustenance. By this time he was living in the city again, with his uncle, a prominent local business owner and former mayor.

Traherne's Puritan upbringing would have been challenged by his education in Oxford, a strongly Royalist city, but appears to have remained basically intact. He studied at Brasenose College, which at this time was itself known for its Evangelical Puritan ethos, taking his first degree in 1657. He later described the delight he took in the range of subjects he was introduced to in this time, revealing 'things in this world of which I never dreamed' and including 'Logic, Ethics, Physics, Metaphysics, Geometry, Astronomy, Poesy, Medicine, Grammar, Music, Rhetoric, all kinds of Arts, Trades and Mechanisms'. He also described how this accumulated learning, for all its richness and insight, left him feeling lacking in the one subject he yearned to master: what he called 'Felicity'. It becomes a word absolutely central to all his subsequent writings, a word which, in the seventeenth century, implied some combination of wisdom, happiness and fulfilment. As he said, 'we studied to inform our knowledge, but knew not for what end we studied', reflecting the heartfelt opinions of university students then and ever after.[88] Leaving Oxford in 1657, Traherne was presented for the living of Credenhill, back home in Herefordshire and thus, at a very young age, took on the duties and responsibilities of being a parish minister. His patrons and advocates were themselves noted Puritans, and his own installation was approved by Cromwell's official committee for such appointments. Traherne settled into his new life with application and genuine commitment. He also continued to cultivate his own spiritual life with renewed intention and a heightened sense of his sacred duty as a minister.

During this time his own views were in an evolutionary process. By 1660, and the restoration of the monarchy and the former polity of the Church of England, he was ready for, and sought, episcopal ordination, well before parish ministers like him were required to do so. In his subsequent writing he defended the established Church of England in its Restoration form with vigour and heartfelt intentionality. This was not merely currying favour. Sometime between 1669 and 1673 he became chaplain to Sir Orlando Bridgeman, the Lord Keeper of the Great Seal, a further sign of his new-found comfort with the establishment. This connection may have come to him because of his friendship back in Herefordshire with Susanna Hopton, the addressee of the *Centuries* and preserver of his works after his death. The chaplaincy came with a post as assistant minister of the parish church in Teddington, where Sir Orlando lived. We do not know how much time Traherne spent there, because he remained as minister in Credenhill too, and indeed was described approvingly by the churchwarden as 'continually resident among us' as late as the year of his death, 1673. But we do know that he was in Teddington when he became ill that year, and that he died in the Bridgeman household. He was buried in the church, beneath the reading desk.

Traherne's mature writing, if we may speak of such of one who died aged 37, might have been entirely lost to posterity, but for some remarkable finds of his manuscripts in the nineteenth and twentieth centuries. During his lifetime he published only *Roman Forgeries*, a polemical work against Catholicism, in 1673. *Christian Ethicks* was published posthumously a couple of years later. The *Centuries of Meditations*, perhaps his masterpiece, were discovered in 1896–7 and published in 1908, at around the same time as his poetic works. In 1997 a further and very early collection, the *Select Meditations*, also finally came to light. Most recently of all, the 'Lambeth' Manuscript has been judged to be a collection of Traherne's writings, including *A Sober View of Dr Twisse*, a theological treatise on Arminian and Calvinist views, and further mystical writings. A number of manuscripts remain unpublished, including *Commentaries of Heaven* and the *Church's Year-Book*, which quotes Andrewes and Herbert among other sources in its evocation of the spirituality of the Christian year. Thomas Traherne was a young man with a great deal to say, who was almost denied the opportunity to say any of it. But for the dedicated work of his most recent researchers and advocates, his exquisite voice would have been lost to us.

At the heart of Traherne's sometimes breathtaking writing is his deep sense of the connectedness of all things created with their Creator. In his description and evocation of this connection, he stands securely in the mystical tradition and in the perhaps surprising company of those like Mother Julian of Norwich and Francis of Assisi, who had had a similar way of seeing and knowing. Traherne's own espousal of this world view, though, is probably also tinged with his enthusiasm for new ways of knowing and new forms of learning that were emerging in England in the seventeenth century and to which he would have been exposed in Oxford. What today we recognize as the scientific method was beginning to come into its own: careful, empirical observation of natural phenomena and an affirmation of the powers of human deduction and reason to make sense of what we see and can measure. Coupled with that, a revival of some Platonic ways of thinking, centred in that other Puritan place of learning, Emmanuel College, Cambridge, was also starting to become influential. The Cambridge Platonists, in their own stress on human reason, were strong advocates of moderation in the midst of the violent divisions of the war. They also stressed, in the face of some Puritan pessimism about human nature and the life of this world generally as fallen and corrupt, the knowability of God, who desires to be encountered by humanity. Nowhere is God's beauty and glory more clearly revealed than in nature. These were ideas that Traherne, in his rural parish, absolutely took to heart.

Indeed, the sense that God wants to be known, and has revealed himself in creation, is the heartbeat of Traherne's *Centuries*, as well as other works. This short summary of human purpose comes towards the beginning of the first book:

> Can you be Holy without accomplishing the end for which you are created? Can you be Divine unless you be Holy? Can you accomplish the end for which you were created, unless you be Righteous? Can you then be Righteous, unless you be just in rendering to Things their due esteem? All things were made to be yours, and you were made to prize them according to their value: which is your office and duty, the end for which you were created, and the means whereby you enjoy. The end for which you were created, is that by prizing all that God hath done, you may enjoy yourself and Him in Blessedness.[89]

Or as he goes on to describe this purpose in relation to the created order:

You never enjoy the world aright, till the Sea itself floweth in your veins, till you are clothed with the heavens, and crowned with the stars: and perceive yourself to be the sole heir of the whole world, and more than so . . .[90]

Commentators have noted that Traherne's 'nature mysticism' prefigures the writing of later authors as diverse as Walt Whitman and Annie Dillard. It is arresting, inventive and endlessly gorgeous. He is firm and even ferocious in his anger against those who fail to enjoy the world and do not value 'the beauty of enjoying it'. If humanity cannot see and find God in the natural order, they will not find God at all. The errors of the human race, he contends, are nowhere more starkly revealed than in its delight in 'gauderies' like jewels and golds, and its concomitant failure to delight in the sun, the sea and the stars. And he has no time at all, probably reflecting the influence of the Cambridge Platonists, for those for whom this earthly life must simply be got through, a gloomy and unremitting preparation for Heaven, where alone they seek ultimate happiness. His understanding of true Christianity is quite different:

There are Christians that place and desire all their happiness in another life, and there is another sort of Christians that desire happiness in this. The one can defer their enjoyment of Wisdom till the World to come, and dispense with the increase and perfection of knowledge for a little time: the other are instant and impatient of delay, and would fain see that happiness here, which they shall enjoy hereafter. Not the vain happiness of this world, falsely called happiness, truly vain: but the real joy and glory of the blessed, which consisteth in the enjoyment of the whole world in communion with God . . . Whether the first sort be Christians indeed, look you to that. They have much to say for themselves. Yet certainly they that put off felicity with long delays are to be much suspected.[91]

Traherne's passionate description of the characteristics of God reflect both previous mystical theology and the particular stream of Anglican thought in which he now found and located himself. There are echoes here of Herbert and Andrewes, whom we know Traherne to have admired. Above all, God is everywhere, and always longing to be found and known by humanity. This omnipresence he describes as pervading 'the life and soul of the universe', with the effect that 'in every point of space from the centre to the heavens, in every kingdom of the world, in every city, in every wilderness, in every house, every soul, every creature, in all the parts of His infinity and eternity' God sees us, loves us, inspires us, and 'crowns' all that we do or accomplish (V:9). Creation is univocal too: in other words, God's voice is consistent. Whether we are absorbed in wonder at the beauty of creation or engrossed in meditating on the life and death of Jesus, we are caught up in the same gospel and the same process of salvation. As Traherne says: 'when I once see that He gave Heaven and Earth to me, and made me in His image to enjoy them . . . I can easily believe that He gave His Son also for me.'[92]

The vivid description of the purity and open-eyed innocence of infancy which so attracted Gerald Finzi comes at a point of the *Centuries* in which Traherne is elucidating his vision of God's intention to speak through nature. It comes therefore as part of a wider discourse about the nature of childhood itself. Traherne does not completely reject the Christian theology of original sin, but he does feel that it is far more a question of nurture than of nature. In this he is resisting and opposing some of the more pessimistic ideas of the Calvinists, famously summarized at the Synod of Dort in 1618–19, whose canons spoke of the 'total depravity' of human nature, even at our entrance into the world, utterly incapable of good. Traherne felt that his own development, as well as reason, suggested otherwise. His delight in nature as a boy was a constant source of joy and delight to him; his experience of human affairs and his assimilation of human traits and frailties was an entirely different matter. It led him to conclude that:

> our misery proceedeth ten thousand times more from the
> outward bondage of opinion and custom, than from any
> inward corruption or deprivation of nature: and that it is not
> our parents' loins, so much as our parents' lives, that enthrals
> and binds us.[93]

Further, it was what he termed 'that burning thirst which Nature
had enkindled in me from my youth' that was his lifeline amid
the later uncertainty and unhappiness that being more deeply
enmeshed in human life and commerce produced. It led him
back to its Creator, whose love was revealed also in the face of
Christ.[94]

Central to Traherne's whole understanding of this is his deeply
mystical insistence on the fundamental unity of God with all that
God has made. He speaks of the image of God in all humanity,
as well as the image of God in all Creation and of the way the
creating Spirit of God is what draws us to nature in reverence
and wonder, and to one another, because it is this same Spirit that
unites us and that we hold in common. His God is profoundly
immanent, present to all in love and mercy. There can be no
separation between the life of the Trinity, active in creation
and redemption, and the life of all God has created, and seeks
to draw back into wholeness with Godself. This seems a bold
claim to some. Traherne, however, resists the severe Calvinist
view of the absolute and irremediable corruption of humanity,
which separates us absolutely from God and cannot be altered
or sanctified. Not only does he resist the notion, he also grounds
his own views firmly in Scripture itself:

> Wisely doth St. John say, *We are the Sons of God* . . . He that
> knoweth not the Spirit of God, can never know a Son of God,
> nor what it is to be His child. He made us the sons of God in
> capacity by giving us a power to see Eternity, to survey His

treasures, to love His children, to know and love as He doth, to become righteous and holy as He is; that we might be blessed and glorious as He is.[95]

This stirring affirmation of the unity of all things finds particular expression in Traherne's writings on the way Jesus, both divine and human, brings the life of Heaven and the life of Earth together. Belief in his person and his purpose, as God's emissary to a world resisting union with its Creator, is transformative in a conflict-ridden, selfish environment. Here Traherne is speaking of the way of life of a wise man, who taught him to see this essential unity and how to act on it. When we act towards others with generosity and grace it is as though Christ were ministering to Christ, a moving picture of the essential unity between and within all living things:

> He thought that he was to treat every man in the person of Christ. That is both as if himself were Christ in the greatness of his love, and also as if the man were Christ, he was to use him having respect to all others. For the love of Christ is to dwell within him, and every man is the object of it. God and he are to become one Spirit, that is one in will, and one in desire. Christ must live within him. He must be filled with the Holy Ghost, which is the God of Love, he must be of the same mind with Christ Jesus, and led by His Spirit. For on the other side he was well acquainted with this mystery – That every man being the object of our Saviour's Love, was to be treated as our Saviour.[96]

Sharing in the humanity of Christ, Christians come to share too in his divinity, witnessed in this kind of living: 'as the fullness of the Godhead dwelleth in our Saviour, it shall dwell in us.'[97]

Fundamental to this divine–human unity too, as he elucidates it, and central to his understanding of the nature of the 'felicity' that he believes to be the goal and purpose of every human life, is the notion of desire or, to use his more seventeenth-century term, 'wanting'. Traherne senses and intuits that our yearning for fulfilment, for happiness, for 'felicity', however we experience it, echoes an even deeper desire in the heart of God: for us. It is both a sign of the image of God within us and the compass that leads back towards God and out of our estrangement from him. Again, this is an idea some find unusual: a God who 'lacks' and yearns for anything. Yet Traherne insists that unless God had been 'full of want', there could have been no creation. In the 'treasure' of all that God has made we see the fulfilment of God's own desire for communion: 'it is incredible, yet very plain'. In the two-way traffic of God's desire for us and our desire for God, we are not only blessed beyond our imagination by discovering God's infinite love for us but also reconnected again to the fundamental union between God and humanity that nothing can ever destroy. Attending to our desires instructs us about what we lack and leads us back to the God who has implanted the desire for communion in us: 'you must want like a God that you may be satisfied like God', as Traherne himself puts it. He goes on:

Wants are the ligatures between God and us, the sinews that convey senses from Him into us, whereby we live in Him, and feels His enjoyments. For had we not been obliged by having our wants satisfied, we should not have been created to love Him. And had we not been created to love Him, we could never have enjoyed His eternal Blessedness.[98]

He expresses the same idea in his poetry:

> For giving me Desire,
> An Eager Thirst, a burning Ardent fire,
> A virgin Infant Flame,
> A Love with which into the World I came,
> An Inward Hidden Heavenly Love,
> Which in my Soul did Work and move,
> And ever ever me Enflame,

With restless longing Heavenly Avarice,
  That never could be satisfied,
That did incessantly a Paradise
  Unknown suggest, and some thing undescried
    Discern, and bear me to it; be
    Thy Name for ever praised by me.[99]

The thread that weaves its way through all of Traherne's writing and mystical theology, very similar to that which can be traced through Herbert's poetry, is his insistence on the nature of God's love for the world. It is a love he sees as essential to the very life and character of the Trinity:

Love loving is the Producer, and that is the Father: Love produced is the Means, and that is the Son: For Love is the means by which a lover loveth. The End of these Means is Love: for it is love by loving: and that is the Holy Ghost. The End and the Producer being both the same, by the Means attained. For by loving Love attaineth itself and being.[100]

Human beings, caught up in the life of God through their enjoyment of nature and their pursuit of their desire for God, participate in this love, both receiving it and sharing it. In this, Traherne asserts that he is no pantheist in his claims about how nature *points* to God; it is but one 'manifestation' of God's love. Indeed, 'the very end for which God made the world, was that He might manifest His Love'; those who cannot be satisfied with the way the world achieves this are unlikely ever to find their desires fulfilled.[101]

More than once Traherne talks of love as God's first and best creation, mirroring the description of the creation of Wisdom in Proverbs 8, whether consciously or not. There, 'Lady Wisdom' describes how she was first-created in order to be God's assistant in the process of creating everything else, and that she remains at God's right hand, overseeing the unfolding life of the world. In his philosophical treatise *The Kingdom of God*, Traherne seems to suggest something rather similar, except that the love of which he speaks so often and so compellingly is now the focus of this language:

> From everlasting he was Infinite, and Eternal Love, and determined to Create the Best of Things: Determining to Create the Best, he created Love: Creating Love he Created the Image of himself; And in that, the Best of all possible things; for Nothing is above the Image of GOD, but God himself. Love is the fellow of Almighty GOD, and fit to be with him for evermore . . . It is the Light of Heaven, the Way to Happiness, the Crown of Rewards, the fulfilling of Laws, and All possessing Treasure: O what Wonder hath He Wrought in Creating Love![102]

Of course, this divine love is also universally experienced and ubiquitous in its scope and extent, something expressed in the *Centuries*, with characteristic passion and beauty of language, in describing how it is 'equally vigorous in all places, equally near to all objects, equally acceptable to all persons, and equally abundant in all its overflowings: Infinitely everywhere'. Further, he reminds his reader, 'this Love is your true self when you are in act what you are in power'; human potential and capacity, as we pursue the fulfilment of our 'wants' and are transformed by our encounter with divine love, is limitless. It is the process by which we make the surprising discovery that we 'are in Heaven everywhere', and need not wait for death for union with God or perfection in love and goodness. We simply need to discover what we already are, by God's love: God's children, made in God's image, to enjoy God's life, here and now.[103]

Even so brief a survey as space allows here illustrates the breadth, vision and grandeur of Thomas Traherne's writings, and of his remarkable understanding of the nature of the Christian life and the character of the Christian God. While rooted in the work of prior authors it is a distinctive and highly personal account of creation and of redemption. Amid the deeply divided context of the country in the mid-seventeenth century, and in the light of a restored Episcopalian Church of England, he stakes a passionate claim for the kind of God he not only believes in but sees revealed in nature and supremely in the life and death of Jesus Christ. God is not punitive; God does not seek revenge; God does not threaten hellfire or seek to save only a predestined few. God is the author, the perpetrator, of an extravagant, costly, universal, other-centred love, a love that does not rest until all that God has made is gathered back again into the fold of that love and into the arms of God. God proceeds in that task by the constant wooing of humanity and a never-ceasing, never-wearying effort of self-giving. The desire of God speaks to the desire of humanity; God's goal is nothing less than the full reconciliation of all things with God's very life.

Although Traherne shares features of his theology and spirituality with other authors, of all denominational identities, there is something quite characteristically Anglican about his approach. After a time of bitter feudal separation, he draws on the positive virtues of moderation and gracious acceptance to offer a riveting picture of an intentionally generous theology. Not only that but he insists on the imperative of the inner life, an ongoing and constant dialogue between the believer and God, an unceasing determination to draw on what a later generation would call 'the means of grace' in order to deepen our encounter with God and experience sanctification in divine love, which alone will offer us the fulfilment of all our desires. As he says in a sort of rule of life in the *Centuries*:

> You must have Glorious Principles implanted in your nature; a clear eye able to see afar off, a great and generous heart, apt to enjoy at any distance: a good and liberal Soul prone to delight in the felicity of all, and an infinite delight to be their Treasure . . . God commandeth you to love all like Him, because He would have you to be His Son, all them to be your riches, you

to be glorious before them, and all the creatures in serving them to be your treasures, while you are His delight, like Him in beauty, and the darling of His bosom.[104]

Like Richard Hooker before him, Thomas Traherne died too young, just as his genius was manifesting itself in sublime theological writing and just as he attained the heights of his own creative powers. His life made little impact in its own time; his works mostly lay unpublished for a further two centuries and more. Today, thanks to the careful work of Traherne scholars, they speak with a vibrancy and relevance to twenty-first-century concerns that is sometimes startling. They certainly illustrate a creative and original mystical theological soul at work. They also show us something rather remarkable, illustrative of what the late Geoffrey Rowell termed the 'Genius of Anglicanism':[105] that a 'middle way' does not need to be a lifeless compromise, with no distinctive contribution to make. Instead, it can hold out a wisdom and a power that is utterly compelling, and commend a way of life that is absolutely transformative amid humanity's jarring discords and warring factions. The contemporary Church, itself bitterly divided and set among a polarized humanity, might profit from reading Traherne again, and learning from him both how to 'enjoy the world aright' and to partake of the life of God. His own prayer for Pentecost pithily sets the trajectory of the Christian life as he envisaged and experienced it:

> Come Holy Ghost Eternal God
> > Our Hearts with Life Inspire
> Inkindle Zeal in all our Souls
> And fill us with thy Heavenly fire.

> Send forth thy Beams, and Let thy Grace
> > Upon my Spirit shine:
> That I may all thy Works enjoy,
> Revive, Sing Praises, be Divine.[106]

Epilogue

In 1967 Gordon Rupp published a slim volume entitled *The Old Reformation and the New*, based on his Cato Lecture from the year before. Reflecting on the themes raised by consideration of the sixteenth century in the light of the Church's situation in the twentieth, and wearied, as he often was, by the tedious letters in the *Church Times* and the *Methodist Recorder*, he wrote of the comfort he had found in the statement on ecumenism of the Second Vatican Council just three years earlier. In particular he highlighted the 'threefold change' that *Unitatis Redintegratio* had pointed to and called for in the Church's life: 'a renewal of its authentic mission and vocation', 'continual Reformation' and 'conversion and change of heart'. He carried on, in words that still have prophetic resonance over 50 years later:

> These things, it is abundantly clear, we can no longer hope to seek or find alone or asunder. One world in revolution needs one Church strong and united, speaking to its condition with the burning charity of Christ Himself. Perhaps this in the end is the one lesson which the reformers have for us. They, too, knew themselves to stand in a dire hour, in utter incompetence and insufficiency. But they knew where to turn and to whom to go. How can a Church be born again when it is old, save in the renewing mercy of Almighty God? Where can it find reformation, save in the Word of Christ who lives and rules? And what is change of heart, but the moving of the Spirit . . ?[107]

Over half a century later the churches' efforts towards unity seem in fact to have moved away from Rupp's optimistic vision, rooted in the confident new stance of the Council. The fear among the denominations about numerical decline is palpable and the congregational statistics are ominous. But Rupp's insight must still hold true. If the Church can do nothing else in these days of insecurity, division, nostalgic longing for a past that probably never existed, and global upheaval, it must find a way to show a frightened world what unity amid difference might look like, and what a Christlike alternative to our own myths, of redemptive violence and the glories of the past, might be. As Rupp reminds us, the reformations of 500 years ago, both Catholic and Protestant, must be a constant, clarion call to us of the truth of the phrase coined by Karl Barth in the wake of the colossal failures of the 1940s: *Ecclesia semper reformanda* – the Church always be in a constant state of being renewed, remade, reshaped, if it is to be the Church.

The figures whose lives and insights have been sketched here point to this too, in their varied and diverse ways, and they show us some common virtues amid their divisions, a hint perhaps of what Rupp was envisaging. Most of them, at some point in their lives, thought that the Church, as they understood the authentic Church to be, was about to die, at least in their own land. All of them met that possibility, and the sense of their own sacred responsibility in the face of discord and serious disagreement, with courage and trust. As Rupp again said in the Cato lectures, we cannot 'gloss over' the sharpness of their rhetoric or the occasional savageness of their prose; but in times very different from ours, with beliefs and understandings sometimes a world removed from ours, they nevertheless embodied some of the qualities of the kind of faith we might desire to be ours. In that, they may offer us hope and purpose. Unlikely as it seems, they may even point us towards unity.

Recently, after Evensong and a very fine dinner in Jesus College, Cambridge, one of the fellows took me up to the Old Library. We ascended in darkness through a bewildering maze of medieval staircases and corridors; he fumbled at a lock in a corner; we moved forward and he felt for a light switch; and we suddenly found ourselves in a room barely altered in 600 years. The real object of our journey was to inspect two surviving books belonging to Thomas Cranmer, somehow rescued from his belongings after his execution and presented to his old college, a tiny fragment of the vast collection we know him to have owned. They were books by humanist Catholics: Erasmus' monumental 1516 translation of the New Testament, the *Novum Instrumentum*, and the massive *Confutation of Tyndale's Answer*, written by Sir Thomas More in 1532 on the eve of King Henry's break with Rome, against the English reformer and Bible translator. It was soon evident that Cranmer was a prolific writer of marginalia: interesting passages were annotated and marked. For really interesting sections he favoured little drawings of pointing fingers, called manicules, executed with delightful detail and apparent fluency.

Surprisingly, there was no polemic: no crossings-out, no scribbled contradictions or angry outbursts. It was possible to imagine him reading with interest, care, deep thought and even delight, noting passages to which he would later wish to return. The experience was somehow profoundly moving: the Archbishop who would reshape the English Church in a dramatically Reformed manner, enjoying the polemical, anti-Evangelical works of his former colleague, who had died for England's union with Rome. This is not the headline of the Reformation nor the image to which we are accustomed. This was instead a glimpse of an entirely different world, and of the passionate, thoughtful, invested human beings who shaped it, more often united in their guiding passions and directing principles than we might suppose – even if the following of those principles and passions, by the light of the faith they had, took them in some divergent directions.

There is a glorious promise at the heart of the New Testament, that no human folly or disaster is so calamitous, wicked or grievous that God, by the divine alchemy of self-giving love described by Herbert and Traherne, cannot transform it for good. It is a gospel promise light years away from the current heretical fad for believing that 'everything happens for a reason', and infinitely more powerful. It is also an essential insight for the modern Church to recover, considering the division it inherits from the Reformation but also from the subsequent centuries of continued fragmentation. Rather than fretting over the question of whether the Church as we know it will die (of course it will – and it must, as the reformers continually remind us), we might rather prayerfully consider how to live honest, open, undefended, passionate, principled Christian lives in these demanding and often terrifying times. Asking that question always leads us in some vastly different directions from merely prioritizing the survival of institutional churches as we have received them. It leads to the courage, the vision, the generosity and the self-denying beauty of the lives we have considered here, at their best. Flawed as we are flawed, they were yet able to give themselves to God's purposes for them, in freedom and trust.

They did so, often in the teeth of fierce opposition and with the real prospect of failure and even death. They did so, sometimes causing harm amid the good they thought and sought to accomplish. But in the miraculous economy of God's life, they did so not in vain. Their inheritance for us, as this book hopes to have shown, is still lively and life-giving. If sometimes the legacy of the Reformation is talked of only in terms of separation, we might think of Thomas Cranmer, poring over the biblical insights of Erasmus or the theology of Thomas More, not wholly agreeing with either but admiring the qualities of both. We should recall the consistent meditations of More too, on his proper Christian duty to those with whom he disagreed. Or picture Katherine Parr, joyfully echoing Thomas à Kempis in the composition of her prayers. We could even spare a thought for Nicholas Harpsfield who, like his friend and Archbishop Reginald Pole, also valued the vision of a Catholic Church that could encompass the breadth of human spiritual experience. And we must think of Matthew Parker, Queen Elizabeth, Lancelot Andrewes, George Herbert or

Thomas Traherne, not only discerning the virtues of a moderate and moderating position but transforming it into a national Church possessed of a distinctive and wholly intentional theology and liturgy, no mere halfway house but a precious gift of wisdom and insight to the global Church.

They also gave their lives not knowing the whole picture or the final outcome but simply trying, through prayerful reflection, to discern what to do next. For all these saints, Catholic and Protestant, the words of another later saint, born Protestant and later converted to Catholicism, might seem apt. Their approach to the tasks ahead of them and to the life to which they sensed God calling them seems very close to his:

> Lead, kindly Light, amid the encircling gloom,
> Lead thou me on;
> The night is dark, and I am far from home,
> Lead thou me on.
> Keep thou my feet; I do not ask to see
> The distant scene; one step enough for me.[108]

From this intimate picture we close with the widest panorama of all, and the question of ultimate purpose and unity. Here again Gordon Rupp has reminded us that we cannot know these things and should not seek to, even though we may have confidence in the final and loving purposes of God. Resolved simply to take the next, faithful step in our pilgrimages of faith, even as the Church seems to endure setback and apparent failure, we keep in mind the one in whose reconciling, universal and unrelenting love all things hold together and will finally be brought to their fullness and purpose:

He was the first Christian, the first Catholic, the first Protestant, the only one who has shared in every part each detail of our separated stories, and who bestrides the future in that wider unity in which, because it is in Him, we shall be at home. For what His people do in memory of Him is a lesser thing than that which He for ever does in His memorial of us – who keeps us in His mind, and bears us on His heart, and offers us together with Himself to the glory of the Eternal Father in the unity of His Body, the fullness of Him who all in all is being fulfilled.[109]

None of those whose lives are glimpsed here, even with all their insight, imagination, creativity and intellectual vigour, could have foreseen a world in which their religious divisions were healed and their lives and faiths reconciled to one another. And yet they faithfully point us to the life of a God with whom all things are possible, in whom all things work together for good and whose ambitious, loving purposes for the renewing of *all* that God has made are never exhausted.

God, which hast prepared to them that love thee such good things as pass all human understanding; pour into our hearts such love toward thee, that we loving thee in all things, may obtain thy promises, which exceed all that we can desire; through Christ our Lord.

Amen.[110]

Notes

1 Gordon Rupp, 1951, *Luther's Progress to the Diet of Worms*, London: SCM Press, p. 53.

2 Jonathan Dean, 2009, *Servitude and Freedom: Reading the Christian Tradition*, Peterborough: Epworth Press.

3 Gordon Rupp, 1967, *The Old Reformation and the New*, London: Epworth Press, pp. 5–8; Rowan Williams, 2004, *Why Study the Past? The Quest for the Historical Church*, London: Darton, Longman & Todd.

4 T. S. Eliot, 1944 and 2001, *Four Quartets*, London: Faber & Faber, p. 36.

5 Eliot, *Four Quartets*, p. 41.

6 Eliot, *Four Quartets*, p. 36.

7 Thomas More (trans. Richardson), 1997, *Utopia*, Ware: Wordsworth, p. 116.

8 Thomas More, 1976, *Complete Works*, Vol. 13, New Haven, CT: Yale University Press, p. 207.

9 Some debate exists among the fellowship of the college about the precise nature of Cranmer's association with it. It is highly likely

he was never actually a fellow: see www.jesus.cam.ac.uk/college/
about-us/history/people-note/thomas-cranmer for more.

10 From a letter to Cromwell answering an opportunistic charge
from Stephen Gardiner that his ancient title of 'Primate of all
England' was an affront to the royal supremacy; quoted in Diarmaid
MacCulloch, 1996, *Thomas Cranmer*, New Haven, CT and London:
Yale University Press, p. 132.

11 Thomas Cranmer (ed. J. Dean), 2012, *God Truly Worshipped*,
Norwich: Canterbury Press, p. 42.

12 Cranmer (ed. Dean), *God Truly Worshipped*, pp. 46–7.

13 Henry Jenkyns, 1833, *The Remains of Thomas Cranmer*, Vol. 2,
Oxford: Oxford University Press, pp. 118–20.

14 Cranmer (ed. Dean), *God Truly Worshipped*, pp. 103–4.

15 Cranmer (ed. Dean), *God Truly Worshipped*, pp. 36–7.

16 'brayds' = 'emotional outbursts'.

17 Cranmer (ed. Dean), *God Truly Worshipped*, pp. 37–9.

18 Jenkyns (ed.), *Remains of Thomas Cranmer*, Vol. 2, p. 157.

19 Cranmer (ed. Dean), *God Truly Worshipped*, p. 158.

20 Nicola Slee, 2004, 'Conversations with Muse', in *Praying Like a
Woman*, London: SPCK, p. 60.

21 See Oliver Wort, 'The Double Life of Anne: John Bale's "Examinations" and "Dive Anne Vitam"', *The Review of English Studies*
Vol. 58, No. 237 (2007), p. 627; Kimberly Anne Coles, 'The Death of

the Author (and the Appropriation of Her Text): The Case of Anne Askew's "Examinations"', *Modern Philology* Vol. 99, No. 4 (2002), pp. 518, 521, 533.

22 Megan Hickerson, 'Negotiating Heresy in Tudor England: Anne Askew and the Bishop of London', *Journal of British Studies* Vol. 46, No. 4 (2007), p. 780.

23 Thomas S. Freeman and Sarah Elizabeth Wall, 'Racking the Body, Shaping the Text: The Account of Annew Askew in Foxe's "Book of Martyrs"', *Renaissance Quarterly* Vol. 54, No. 4, Part 1 (2001).

24 Diane Watt, 2001, *Secretaries of God*, Cambridge: D. S. Brewer, p. 117.

25 Frederick H. Shriver, Review of 'John Bale: Mythmaker for the English Reformation' by Leslie P. Fairfield, *Historical Magazine of the Protestant Episcopal Church* Vol. 47, No. 4 (1978), pp. 487–8.

26 Quoted in Watt, *Secretaries of God*, p. 84.

27 Disagreement here with Theresa D. Kemp ('Translating Anne Askew: The Textual Remains of a Sixteenth-Century Heretic and Saint', *Renaissance Quarterly* Vol. 52, No. 4 (1999), p. 1030) and Watt, *Secretaries of God* (pp. 103–4), who notices similarities with Catherine et al. but perhaps ought to consider why Bale does not explicitly draw on them. The fact that he does not rather undermines her case for a continuum between medieval and early modern sensibilities here.

28 Elaine V. Beilin (ed.), 1996, *The Examinations of Anne Askew*, New York and Oxford: Oxford University Press, pp. 77–8, 86.

29 John N. King, 'The Godly Woman in Elizabethan Iconography', *Renaissance Quarterly* Vol. 38, No. 1 (1985), p. 54.

30 Wort, 'The Double Life of Anne', pp. 637–8.

31 Watt, *Secretaries of God*, p. 107; Beilin (ed.), *Examinations of Anne Askew*, pp. 9–11.

32 Beilin (ed.), *Examinations*, pp. 19–20, 48.

33 Beilin (ed.), *Examinations*, pp. 24, 27, 92.

34 Beilin (ed.), *Examinations*, pp. 29–30, 94–5.

35 Beilin (ed.), *Examinations*, pp. 32–4, 42–4.

36 Beilin (ed.), *Examinations*, pp. 39–40, 97, 120.

37 Beilin (ed.), *Examinations*, p. 56.

38 Beilin (ed.), *Examinations*, p. 126.

39 Beilin (ed.), *Examinations*, pp. 129–30.

40 Freeman and Wall, 'Racking the Body, Shaping the Text', pp. 1180–1, 1191; L. P. Fairfield, 1976, *John Bale: Mythmaker for the English Reformation*, West Lafayette, IN: Purdue University Press; emphasis in original.

41 Wesley (ed.), 1819, *The Christian Library*, Vol. 2, London: T. Cordeux, pp. 3–4, 419–21; emphasis in original.

42 Nicola Slee, 2011, *Seeking the Risen Christa*, London: SPCK.

43 Katherine Parr, 1831, *Prayers and Meditations*, London: Religious Tract Society, p. 25.

44 Parr, *Prayers and Meditations*, p. 16.

45 Parr, *Prayers and Meditations*, p. 22.

46 Katherine Parr, 1831, *The Lamentation of a Sinner*, London: Religious Tract Society, p. 43.

47 Parr, *Lamentation of a Sinner*, p. 63.

48 Nicholas Harpsfield (ed. Hitchcock), 1932, *The Life and Death of Sir Thomas More*, Oxford: Early English Text Society, p. 169.

49 Nicholas Harpsfield (ed. Houghton), 1877–84, *Bishop Cranmer's Recantacyons*, London: Philobiblion Society.

50 Nicholas Harpsfield, 1566, *Dialogi Sex*, Antwerp, p. 766.

51 Matthew Parker (ed. Bruce), 1853, *Correspondence*, Cambridge: Cambridge University Press, p. 57.

52 Parker, *Correspondence*, p. 68.

53 Parker, *Correspondence*, p. 17.

54 A fourth son was born in 1556, during Mary's reign, but did not survive.

55 Parker, *Correspondence*, p. viii.

56 Parker, *Correspondence*, pp. 223–7.

57 That is, he will gladly take the unpopularity for merely enforcing the Queen's orders.

58 Parker, *Correspondence*, p. 237.

59 Parker, *Correspondence*, p. 235.

60 Parker, *Correspondence*, pp. 478–9.

61 Taken from www.papalencyclicals.net/Pius05/p5regnans.htm (29 May 2017).

62 Most scholars prefer now to speak simply of a 'Catholic Reformation' in the sixteenth century, to demonstrate continuity with movements from before Luther (e.g. the Christian humanism of Erasmus and More) and to recall that all was not simply a response to the Protestant challenge.

63 Referenced at www.gutenberg.org/cache/epub/13133/pg13133.html (30 May 2017).

64 From Leah Marcus, Janel Mueller and Mary Beth Rose (eds), 2000, *Elizabeth I: Collected Works*, Chicago: University of Chicago Press, pp. 319–21.

65 H. R. McAdoo, 1965, *The Spirit of Anglicanism: A Survey of Anglican Theological Method in the Seventeenth Century*, London: A. & C. Black, p. 329.

66 The Latin of Psalm 2.7, 'this day I have begotten you'.

67 Sermon XVI of the Resurrection, in the *Ninety-Six Sermons* of 1874, Vol. 3, pp. 58–9 and reproduced in Rowell, Stevenson and Williams (eds), 2001, *Love's Redeeming Work: The Anglican Quest for Holiness*, Oxford: Oxford University Press, pp. 116–17.

68 Whitsun Sermon III, reproduced in Raymond Chapman (ed.), 2008, *Before the King's Majesty: Lancelot Andrewes and His Writings*, Norwich: Canterbury Press, pp. 97–8.

69 Nativity Sermon XV, reproduced in Chapman (ed.), *Before the King's Majesty*, pp. 27–8.

70 F. E. Brightman (ed.), 1903, *The Preces Privatae of Lancelot Andrewes*, London: Methuen, pp. 198, 235, 273.

71 George Herbert (ed. Ann Pasternak Slater), 1995, *The Complete English Works*, London: Everyman, pp. 86–7.

72 Herbert, *Complete English Works*, pp. 156–7.

73 Quoted in Geoffrey Rowell, Kenneth Stevenson and Rowan Williams (eds), 2001, *Love's Redeeming Work: The Anglican Quest for Holiness*, Oxford: Oxford University Press, pp. 163, 165–6.

74 Herbert, *Complete English Works*, pp. 108–9.

75 Herbert, *Complete English Works*, pp. 61–2.

76 Herbert, *Complete English Works*, pp. 149–50.

77 Herbert, *Complete English Works*, pp. 149–50.

78 Taken from George Herbert (ed. Ann Pasternak Slater), 1995, *The Complete English Works*, London: Everyman, p. 361.

79 Justin Lewis-Anthony's book, *If You Meet George Herbert on the Road, Kill Him: Radically Re-Thinking Priestly Ministry*, London: Mowbray, 2009, is a very useful and thoughtful manual on twenty-first-century priesthood, but reflects a certain excess in its rejection of Herbert's methods (even if it actually says complimentary things about him).

80 Herbert, *Complete English Works*, pp. 84–5.

81 Herbert, *Complete English Works*, p. 49.

82 Herbert, *Complete English Works*, pp. 174–5.

NOTES

83 Herbert, *Complete English Works*, p. 37.

84 Herbert, *Complete English Works*, p. 120.

85 Herbert, *Complete English Works*, pp. 153–4.

86 Herbert, *Complete English Works*, p. 82.

87 Thomas Traherne (ed. Bertram Dobell), 1960, *Centuries*, London: Faith Press. In this extract from the text of his *Dies Natalis*, Finzi selects and rearranges passages freely from numbers 1 and 2 of the Third Century.

88 Traherne, *Centuries* III, nos 35–37, pp. 129–30.

89 Traherne, *Centuries* I, no. 12, pp. 6–7.

90 Traherne, *Centuries* I, no. 29, p. 14.

91 Traherne, *Centuries* IV, no. 9, pp. 171–2.

92 Traherne, *Centuries* II, no. 6, pp. 227–8, 59.

93 Traherne, *Centuries* III, no. 8, p. 114.

94 Traherne, *Centuries* III, no. 46, pp. 114, 135.

95 Traherne, *Centuries* I, no. 99, p. 52.

96 Traherne, *Centuries* IV, no. 28, p. 180.

97 Traherne, *Centuries* IV, no. 100, p. 219.

98 Traherne, *Centuries* I, no. 51, pp. 20, 24.

99 Thomas Traherne (ed. Denise Inge), 2008, *Happiness and Holiness: Thomas Traherne and his Writings*, Norwich: Canterbury Press, p. 130.

100 Traherne, *Centuries* II, no. 46, pp. 78–9.

101 Traherne, *Centuries* II, no. 85, pp. 78–9, 85.

102 Traherne, *Happiness and Holiness*, pp. 182–3.

103 Traherne, *Centuries* IV, nos 38, 66, pp. 183, 199.

104 Traherne, *Centuries* I, nos 38–39, pp. 18–19.

105 Geoffrey Rowell (ed.), 1992, *The English Religious Tradition and the Genius of Anglicanism*, Wantage: Ikon.

106 From the *Church's Year-Book* (unpublished), quoted in Traherne, *Happiness and Holiness*, pp. 299–300.

107 Gordon Rupp, 1967, *The Old Reformation and the New*, London: Epworth Press, pp. 66–7.

108 Written by John Henry Newman in 1833, during a time of illness and vocational uncertainty.

109 Gordon Rupp, 1960, *Protestant Catholicity: Two Lectures*, London: Epworth Press, pp. 55–6.

110 Collect for the Sixth Sunday after Trinity.

Index of Names

INDEX OF NAMES

CPSIA information can be obtained
at www.ICGtesting.com
Printed in the USA
BVHW071137281018
531381BV00001BA/114/P